VIEWPOINT

Student's Book 2B

Michael McCarthy
Jeanne McCarten
Helen Sandiford

CAMBRIDGE
UNIVERSITY PRESS

University Printing House, Cambridge CB2 8BS, United Kingdom

One Liberty Plaza, 20th Floor, New York, NY 10006, USA

477 Williamstown Road, Port Melbourne, VIC 3207, Australia

314–321, 3rd Floor, Plot 3, Splendor Forum, Jasola District Centre, New Delhi – 110025, India

79 Anson Road, #06–04/06, Singapore 079906

Cambridge University Press is part of the University of Cambridge.

It furthers the University's mission by disseminating knowledge in the pursuit of education, learning and research at the highest international levels of excellence.

www.cambridge.org
Information on this title: www.cambridge.org/9781107601550

© Cambridge University Press 2016

This publication is in copyright. Subject to statutory exception and to the provisions of relevant collective licensing agreements, no reproduction of any part may take place without the written permission of Cambridge University Press.

Student's Book first published 2014
Online Course 2016

20 19 18 17 16 15 14 13 12 11 10 9 8 7 6 5

Printed in Great Britain by CPI Group (UK) Ltd, Croydon CR0 4YY

A catalog record for this publication is available from the British Library.

ISBN 978-0-521-13189-6 Student's Book
ISBN 978-1-107-60154-3 Student's Book A
ISBN 978-1-107-60155-0 Student's Book B
ISBN 978-1-107-60631-9 Workbook
ISBN 978-1-107-57205-8 Workbook A
ISBN 978-1-107-57213-3 Workbook B
ISBN 978-1-107-60156-7 Teacher's Edition with Assessment Audio CD/CD-ROM
ISBN 978-1-107-66132-5 Class Audio CDs (4)
ISBN 978-1-107-67577-3 Presentation Plus
ISBN 978-1-107-56841-9 Student's Book with Online Workbook
ISBN 978-1-107-56846-4 Student's Book with Online Workbook A
ISBN 978-1-107-56849-5 Student's Book with Online Workbook B
ISBN 978-1-107-56808-2 Student's Book with Online Course (includes Online Workbook)
ISBN 978-1-107-56809-9 Student's Book with Online Course (includes Online Workbook) A
ISBN 978-1-107-56810-5 Student's Book with Online Course (includes Online Workbook) B

Additional resources for this publication at www.cambridge.org/viewpoint

Cambridge University Press has no responsibility for the persistence or accuracy of URLs for external or third-party internet websites referred to in this publication, and does not guarantee that any content on such websites is, or will remain, accurate or appropriate.

Authors' acknowledgements

The authors would like to thank the entire team of professionals who have contributed their expertise to creating *Viewpoint 2*. We appreciate you all, including those we have not met. Here we would like to thank the people with whom we have had the most personal, day-to-day contact through the project. In particular, Michael Poor, who skillfully and sensitively edited the material and dedicated so much time and professional expertise to help us improve it; Mary Vaughn for her usual sage advice on our syllabus and her excellent contributions to the pronunciation materials; Dawn Elwell for her superb production skills; copy editor Karen Davy for checking through the manuscripts; Sue Aldcorn and Arley Gray for their work on creating the Teacher's Edition; Helen Tiliouine, Therese Naber and Janet Gokay, for creating and editing the testing program; Cristina Zurawski and Graham Skerritt for their comments on some of the early drafts, Mary McKeon, for her series oversight and project management; Melissa Struck for her help on the workbook and project management; Rossita Fernando and Jennifer Pardilla for their roles on the Workbook, Class Audio, and Video Program; Catherine Black for her support on the answer keys and audio scripts and deft handling of the Online Workbook; Tyler Heacock and Kathleen Corley, and their friends and family for the recordings they made, which fed into the materials; Ann Fiddes for corpus support and access to the English Profile wordlists; Dr. Cynan Ellis Evans for the interview on page 45, and Kristen Ulmer for the interview which is reported on page 55.

We would also like to express our deep appreciation to Bryan Fletcher and Sarah Cole, who started the *Viewpoint* project with incredible vision and drive; and Janet Aitchison for her continued support.

Finally, we would like to thank each other for getting through another project together! In addition, Helen Sandiford would like to thank her husband, Bryan, and her daughters for their unwavering support.

In addition, a great number of people contributed to the research and development of *Viewpoint*. The authors and publishers would like to extend their particular thanks to the following for their valuable insights and suggestions.

Reviewers and consultants:
Elisa Borges and Samara Camilo Tomé Costa from **Instituto Brasil-Estados Unidos**, Rio de Janeiro, Brazil; Deborah Iddon from **Harmon Hall** Cuajimalpa, México; and Chris Sol Cruz from **Suncross Media LLC**. Special thanks to Sedat Cilingir, Didem Mutçalıoğlu, and Burcu Tezvan from **İstanbul Bilgi Üniversitesi**, İstanbul, Turkey for their invaluable input in reviewing both the Student's Book and Workbook.

The authors and publishers would also like to thank our design and production teams at Nesbitt Graphics, Inc., Page 2, LLC, and New York Audio Productions.

Cambridge University Press staff and advisors:
Mary Lousie Baez, Jeff Chen, Seil Choi, Vincent Di Blasi, Julian Eynon, Maiza Fatureto, Keiko Hirano, Chris Hughes, Peter Holly, Tomomi Katsuki, Jeff Krum, Christine Lee, John Letcher, Vicky Lin, Hugo Loyola, Joao Madureira, Alejandro Martinez, Daniela A. Meyer, Devrim Ozdemir, Jinhee Park, Gabriela Perez, Panthipa Rojanasuworapong, Luiz Rose, Howard Siegelman, Satoko Shimoyama, Ian Sutherland, Alicione Soares Tavares, Frank Vargas, Julie Watson, Irene Yang, Jess Zhou, Frank Zhu.

Viewpoint Level 2B *Scope and sequence*

	Functions / Topics	Grammar	Vocabulary	Conversation strategies	Speaking naturally
Unit 7 **Relationships** pages 74–83	• Talk about relationships, marriage, and family life. • Discuss the most important issues to consider before getting married. • Talk about the best ways to meet people. • Evaluate the pros and cons of monitoring family members.	• Use conditional sentences without *if* to hypothesize. • Use *wh-* clauses as subjects and objects.	• Binomial expressions with *and, or, but* (*give and take, sooner or later, slowly but surely*) • Building synonyms (*see – perceive; improve – enhance*)	• Use expressions like *in the end* and *in a word* to summarize or finish your points. • Use *then* and *in that case* to draw a conclusion from something someone said.	• Binomial pairs *page 141*
Unit 8 **History** pages 84–93	• Talk about people and events in history. • Determine what makes a historical event "world-changing." • Talk about the importance of one's family history.	• Use the perfect infinitive to refer to past time. • Use cleft sentences beginning with *It* to focus on certain nouns, phrases, and clauses.	• Adjective antonyms (*lasting – temporary; superficial – profound*) • Metaphors (*sift, bring to life*)	• Use expressions like *Let's not go there* to avoid talking about a topic. • Respond with *That's what I'm saying* to focus on your viewpoint.	• Saying perfect infinitives *page 141*
Unit 9 **Engineering wonders** pages 94–103	• Talk about feats, challenges, and developments in engineering. • Evaluate the priorities in research and development. • Discuss the usefulness of robots.	• Use *-ever* words in talking about unknown people or things. • Use negative adverbs (*never, not only*) + inversion to start a sentence for emphasis.	• Vocabulary of engineering projects (*erect, install*) • Verbs (*interact, determine*)	• Use expressions like *given* or *considering* to introduce facts that support your opinions. • Emphasize negative phrases with *at all* and *whatsoever*.	• Intonation of background information *page 142*

Checkpoint 3 Units 7–9 pages 104-105

Listening	Reading	Writing	Vocabulary notebook	Grammar extra
Bringing up baby? • A student talks about his experience with a "baby simulator." *Keeping tabs on the family* • A family counselor discusses using technology to keep track of family members.	*Technology – is it driving families apart?* • An article about how technology impacts family dynamics	• Write a magazine article about how to enhance friendships. • Express number and amount with expressions like *a number of, a great deal of*. • Avoid errors with *a number of*, etc. • Use expressions like *affect, have an effect on* to describe effects.	*Now or never* • Use expressions in sentences that are personally meaningful.	• More on inversions • More on *what* clauses • *what* clauses with passive verbs and modals in writing *pages 156–157*
Tracing family histories • Two friends talk about their family backgrounds. *Citizen participation projects* • A lecturer describes projects that help uncover the past.	*The Ancient Lives Project* • An article about the collaboration between experts and volunteers in piecing together the past	• Write a narrative essay about your family or someone you know. • Order events in the past. • Avoid errors with *in the end* and *at the end*.	*Deep, low, high* • Look up the synonyms and antonyms of new words.	• More on perfect infinitives • The perfect infinitive after adjectives and nouns • More on cleft sentences with *it + be* • *it + be* + noun phrase in writing *pages 158–159*
Other amazing feats • Three documentaries describe marvels of engineering. *Is she for real?* • A radio interview about a robot.	*Robots* • An article about the widespread use of robots in society	• Write an essay about whether robots can replace humans. • Express alternatives. • Avoid errors with *would rather / rather than*.	*How do you do it?* • Ask yourself questions using new vocabulary.	• *whatever, whichever,* and *whoever* as subjects and objects • Patterns with *however* and *whatever* • More on inversion • Inversion with modals and in passive sentences *pages 160–161*

Checkpoint 3 Units 7–9   pages 104-105

Scope and sequence

	Functions / Topics	Grammar	Vocabulary	Conversation strategies	Speaking naturally
Unit 10 **Current events** pages 106–115	• Talk about the news, who reports it, and how. • Discuss if speed or accuracy is more important in news reporting. • Evaluate how much you trust what you hear or read in the news.	• Use continuous infinitive forms to report events in progress. • Use the subjunctive to describe what should happen, what is important, and to refer to demands and recommendations.	• Noun and verb collocations (*undergo surgery, contain an oil spill*) • Vocabulary to express truth or fiction (*verify, fabricate*)	• Highlight topics by putting them at the start or end of what you say. • Use *this* and *these* to highlight information and *that* and *those* to refer to known information.	• Stress and intonation *page 142*
Unit 11 **Is it real?** pages 116–125	• Talk about whether information is true or not. • Consider how you would handle an emergency. • Talk about white lies and if they're ever acceptable. • Discuss if art forgers are still true artists.	• Use *be to* to refer to fixed or hypothetical future events. • Use passive verb complements.	• Idioms and phrasal verbs with *turn* (*turn over a new leaf, turn around*) • Words in context (*lucrative, laborious*)	• Use expressions like *That doesn't seem right* to express concerns. • Use *to me, to her*, etc. to introduce an opinion.	• Stress in longer idioms *page 143*
Unit 12 **Psychology** pages 126–135	• Talk about being independent, the psychology of attraction, and the brain. • Discuss the differences between online and in-person relationships. • Discuss stereotypes.	• Use objects + *-ing* forms after prepositions and verbs. • Use reflexive pronouns — including to add emphasis — and *each other / one another*.	• Phrasal verbs (*go by, pick up on*) • Expressions with *be, do, go, have, take* (*be close to, have to do with*)	• Use expressions like *I can see it from both sides* and *by the same token*. • Use *to put it* + adverb to indicate your meaning behind an opinion.	• Stress with reflexive pronouns *page 143*

Checkpoint 4 Units 10–12 pages 136-137

Scope and sequence

Listening	Reading	Writing	Vocabulary notebook	Grammar extra
Journalism • A guest on a radio program discusses trends in journalism.	*Establishing the truth: How accurate are news reports?* • An article about issues in news reporting	• Summarize an article. • Use subject-verb agreement. • Avoid subject-verb agreement errors in relative clauses.	*Trust your instincts* • Find multiple verbs that collocate with the same noun.	• Simple vs. continuous infinitives • More on perfect continuous infinitives • More on the subjunctive • The subjunctive and conditional sentences *pages 162–163*
Online lies • Two friends talk about the lies that people tell about themselves online. *Fakes of art!* • A radio program profiles artist John Myatt.	*Authenticating art* • An article about the techniques used to identify art forgeries	• Write an essay about fake designer goods. • Share your views and those of others. • Use academic conjunctions and adverbs. • Avoid errors with *provided that*.	*Use it or lose it.* • Use new vocabulary in imaginary conversations with a friend.	• More on *be to; be due to, be meant to* • *be to* for orders and instructions • More on passive perfect infinitives • *would rather* *pages 164–165*
"Helicopter" parents • A mother and son talk about overprotective parents. *Understanding the brain – outcomes* • Four professionals lecture about the impact of brain research on their fields.	*The developing brain* • An article about how brain development relates to behavior	• Write a report using statistics. • Compare statistics. • Use expressions like *twice as likely, four times more often*. • Avoid errors with *twice*.	*Pick and choose* • Create a thesaurus.	• Common verbs, adjectives, and nouns + object + *-ing* • More on reflexive pronouns • Referring to unknown people *pages 166–167*

Checkpoint 4 Units 10–12   pages 136-137

Scope and sequence 7

Unit 7

Relationships

In Unit 7, you . . .
- talk about relationships, marriage, and family life.
- express the idea of *if* in different ways.
- use *wh-* clauses as subjects and objects to focus information.
- finish a point with expressions like *in the end*.
- say *then* and *in that case* in responses to draw a conclusion.

Lesson A Parenting

1 Grammar in context

A What's the best age to become a parent? Tell the class your views.

B CD 3.02 Listen to the podcast. What's the speaker's main proposal about parenting?

STATIONS • ABOUT • SUPPORT • LOG IN • SIGN UP

PODCAST LISTEN LIVE SHARE

Our Family Season continues with Rachel Birken's take on the topic of parenting.

A friend of mine struggling with sleepless nights after the birth of her daughter recently said to me, quote, "Had I known having a baby would be this hard, I might have waited a few more years. Why aren't parenting classes mandatory, especially in high school?" Which got me thinking: Why *aren't* they?

Ask any new parent this question: "Would you have benefited from parenting classes?" and you'll probably get the answer, "Absolutely!" Most parents experience problems with sleepless nights, anxiety about their baby's health, and as their children grow, issues with behavior and setting boundaries. Should you think your experience will be any different, think again. Parenting is a skill to be learned.

Some school districts have recognized this and introduced programs where students take care of a computerized baby doll that behaves like a real baby. It cries in the night and needs to be changed and comforted. It helps young people understand what is involved in starting a family.

One college senior I know who did this told me it was a cool experience and that had he not taken that class, he wouldn't have realized what hard work a baby is.

Were I in charge of education, I would make all students from the age of 12 do this for a whole weekend every year.

Should you need further evidence that parenting classes are a good idea, school and city districts all over the country are expanding programs that offer workshops in parenting skills – not to students – but to *parents* of their students. Clearly, there is a need out there.

So let's make parenting classes mandatory. Otherwise, we run the risk of creating a generation of parents who are unprepared to tackle the most important job of their lives.

C **Pair work** Discuss the questions.
- What reasons does the speaker give or imply for her proposal? What are they?
- What gave her the idea in the first place?
- How does the baby doll program work? What is its goal?
- Why do you think parenting classes are offered by city and school districts?

74 Unit 7: Relationships

2 Grammar Hypothesizing

Figure it out

A Rewrite these phrases without *If*. Use the podcast to help you. Then read the grammar chart.

1. If you ask any new parent this question, . . .
2. If I had known having a baby would be this hard, . . .
3. If you need further evidence that parenting classes are needed, . . .
4. If we don't do this, we run the risk . . .

Conditional sentences without *if*

Grammar extra See page 156.

You can use these structures to introduce a hypothetical idea without using the word *if*.

Imperative . . . and . . .	**Ask** any new parent the question, **and** you'll get the answer, "Absolutely!"
Inversions *Were* + subject (+ infinitive) *Had* + subject + past participle *Should* + subject + verb	**Were I** in charge of education, I would make this class mandatory. **Were she** to have another baby, she would be better prepared. **Had I known** it would be this hard, I would have waited. **Should you think** your experience will be any different, think again.
Otherwise	Let's make them mandatory. **Otherwise**, parents will be unprepared.

Writing vs. Conversation
Inversions are much more common in writing and formal speaking than in conversation.

B Change the *if* clauses, using the words or structure given.

Had I had

1. ~~If I had~~ the chance to take care of a doll in school, I would have said, "No way." (*Had*)
2. If I were to become a school principal, I would make parenting classes mandatory. (*Were*)
3. If you make parenting classes mandatory, students will hate them. (imperative)
4. If I were to become a parent in the next year, I'd be very happy. (*Were*)
5. If you ask most kids what it's like to have children, they'll say, "It's easy." (imperative)
6. Teaching kids about relationships is a good idea. If we don't, how do they learn? (*Otherwise*)
7. I'd want my kids to take other "life" classes like personal finance, if that were possible. (*should*)
8. If I had known more about life when I left school, things would have been easier. (*Had*)

About you

C **Pair work** Do you agree with the sentences above? Change them to express your own views.

"Had I had the chance to take care of a doll in high school, I would have done it."

3 Listening and speaking Bringing up baby?

A 🔊 CD 3.03 Listen. What was Brandon's class? Was it a positive experience?

B 🔊 CD 3.04 Listen again. Are the sentences true or false? Write T or F. Then correct the false sentences.

1. It was a mandatory class. ____
2. He knew before he did it how hard it would be. ____
3. He found changing diapers the worst part. ____
4. It taught him how much time a baby needs. ____
5. His friends said how annoying it was to do. ____
6. He's not sure if it's a good idea for his age group. ____

About you

C **Pair work** Agree on four classes you would make mandatory to help students prepare for life.

Unit 7: Relationships 75

Lesson B *Questions to ask*

1 Vocabulary in context

A **CD 3.05** What issues do you think couples should discuss and agree on before they get married? Make a list. Then read the article. Which of your ideas are mentioned?

Getting married? *Don't just wait and see what happens.*

So you've met the man or woman of your dreams and decided to become **husband and wife**. You're probably **sick and tired** of reading the divorce statistics, but they're not encouraging. In many Western countries, around 40 percent of marriages end in divorce. Why divorce rates are so high is not clear. But what many couples fail to do is to discuss the important issues before the wedding. So, **stop and think** now – you'll save yourself **time and energy** and maybe avoid a lot of **pain and suffering**.

MONEY
Is how you spend money a problem right now? When you're married, it will likely become a problem **sooner or later**. Agree now on how much you will spend – for example, on rent, vacations, entertainment, etc. – and what your financial goals are. Do you know if you'll keep separate bank accounts?

WORK
How many hours a week you work can be an issue. Tell each other now if you intend to work **above and beyond** a normal workweek; otherwise, **slowly but surely** those long hours will cause resentment. Discuss whether or not you would both move to another city because of work. How would you feel were your partner to work away from home and commute **back and forth** on weekends?

CONFLICTS
Every relationship has its **ups and downs**, but **in this day and age**, marriage is all about **give-and-take**. How you resolve differences can be critical and may predict the **success or failure** of a marriage. Can you agree without arguing how often your in-laws can visit?

You can't always **pick and choose** where you **live and work**, but can you compromise should you have different views?   [MORE...]

About you

B Complete the expressions with words from the article. Then discuss the comments with a partner. Do you agree with the views given?

1. I know that divorce causes a lot of pain _____, but it takes a lot of time _____ to discuss these questions, too. I think you should just get married if you want to and then wait _____ what happens.
2. I don't think people stop _____ before getting married. There are a lot more things to agree on above _____ the ideas in the article.
3. Sooner _____ everyone argues. You can't avoid it as husband _____.
4. All couples have their ups _____. You can't agree on everything, so pick _____ what you argue about.
5. I agree marriage is about give _____, but I like to get my own way, and slowly _____ I usually do.
6. In this day _____, we don't need advice about marriage. I'm sick _____ of reading articles like this.
7. It's not a problem to live _____ in two places. It'd be fun to travel back _____.

Word sort

C Make a chart of the expressions in bold in the article. Add more ideas.

and	but	or
wait and see		

Vocabulary notebook
See page 83.

Unit 7: Relationships

2 Grammar Information focus

Figure it out

A Underline the sentences in the article with these meanings.

1. How do you spend money? Is it a problem right now?
2. Why are divorce rates high? It's not clear.
3. Will you keep separate bank accounts? Do you know?
4. Where do you live and work? You can't always pick and choose.

Wh– clauses as subjects and objects

Grammar extra See page 157.

A *wh–* clause can be the subject or object of a verb. Using a *wh–* clause as the subject gives extra emphasis to it. Notice the statement word order in the *wh–* clause.

Subjects
Is **how you spend money** a problem right now?
What many couples fail to do is (to) discuss the important issues.
How you resolve differences can be critical.

Objects
Can you agree **how often your partner's family can visit** without arguing?
Tell each other now **whether / if you intend to work long hours**.
Agree now on **what your financial goals are**.

> **In conversation . . .**
> You can also say *whether or not* when there is a choice of two options.
> Discuss **whether or not** you would both move to another city.

B Rewrite the two sentences as one sentence. Keep the clauses in the same order.

1. Should you tell your husband or wife this? Which of his or her friends don't you like?
   Should you tell your husband or wife which of his or her friends you don't like?
2. Why do couples divorce? It's usually obvious, don't you think?
3. How many hours a week do you work? It can easily become a problem, can't it?
4. It's important to discuss this. Do you both want children?
5. You should also decide this. How many children do you both want to have?
6. You need to find this out. Does your partner have different religious or political views?
7. Who does the chores? This will become an issue sooner or later.
8. Is it important to decide this? How often will you go out separately with your own friends?

About you

C **Pair work** Discuss the questions and statements above. Do you have the same views?

3 Viewpoint A manifesto for marriage

Pair work Discuss the 10 most important issues you need to agree on before you get married. Use these ideas and add your own.

| chores | money | visiting in-laws |
| leisure time | raising children | work |

A How you spend money is the first thing to discuss, I would say.
B Yes. It seems to me you should agree on what you spend money on.

> **In conversation . . .**
> You can soften opinions with *I would say, I would think, I would imagine,* and *It seems to me*.

See page 141

Lesson C *In the end*

1 Conversation strategy Finishing a point

A ◆ CD 3.06 What are the advantages and disadvantages of Internet dating sites? Make a list. Then listen. What do Tara and Carmen think about them?

Tara	Did I tell you I'm going out on a date tonight?
Carmen	No. Who with?
Tara	This guy I met on an Internet dating site.
Carmen	Is that . . . all right?
Tara	Oh, yeah. Talk to anybody these days, and you'll probably find they're using dating sites.
Carmen	So you think it's OK, then?
Tara	I do. Really and truly. It's just like being at a party. You see somebody you like, you arrange to meet and –
Carmen	But you don't *really* know who they are. I mean, when all's said and done, surely it's better to get to know them a little first.
Tara	Well, you do. You email or call. It's so convenient. And in the end, you don't waste time on people you're not interested in.
Carmen	I guess.
Tara	You know, all the time I spend working, I'll never meet anybody otherwise.
Carmen	Well, in that case, do you have time to date? I mean, at the end of the day, if you're always working, you probably don't have time for a boyfriend.

B **Notice** how Carmen and Tara summarize and finish their points with expressions like these. Find examples in the conversation.

> at the end of the day   in a word
> in the end   in a nutshell
> when all's said and done

In conversation . . .
The most common expressions are *in the end* and *at the end of the day*. In writing, you can use *in a word* and *in a nutshell* or the more formal *in the final analysis*.

About you

C ◆ CD 3.07 Listen. Complete Tara's comments with the expressions you hear. Then discuss the views with a partner. Do you agree with her?

1. People don't go out to meet people – it takes time. _____, we're all too busy.
2. I read an academic article about Internet dating that said, "Online daters are just like face-to-face daters. _____, there is no difference between them."
3. You can email and call or video chat before you first meet. So really, _____, you're already friends.
4. You don't need to go out and spend money on movies or restaurants. _____, it's a lot cheaper.
5. And because you do it from home, you don't get into difficult situations. _____, it's safer, too.
6. There are lots of people that you can get to know online. _____ , you don't have to choose just one.

Unit 7: Relationships

2 Strategy plus ..., then

🔊 CD 3.08 You can end a response with **then** to draw a conclusion from what someone just said.

So you think it's OK, **then**?

You can also say **In that case**, which means "because of what was just said."

In conversation . . .

In that case usually comes near the beginning of what people say.

A Match the comments with the responses. Write the letters a–f. Then practice in pairs.

1. Some research shows that 94 percent of online daters go out more than once. _____
2. Apparently, only 5 percent of people who use online dating actually establish a relationship. _____
3. Online daters prefer instant messaging to email because it's more like a real conversation. _____
4. They tend not to use their webcams, though. _____
5. What a lot of people do is to email or chat for weeks before they actually meet. _____
6. Look at the people using Internet dating sites, and you'll find mostly middle-aged people. _____

a. That's interesting. Email isn't considered a good way to get to know somebody, then.
b. Well, in that case, you've got a good chance of getting at least a couple of dates.
c. OK, so in that case, what do they have to talk about when they get together?
d. So it's not just young people, then?
e. Well, in that case, it doesn't have a very high success rate, then, does it?
f. So in that case, you don't need to look your best when you're dating online.

About you | **B** Pair work Take turns reading the comments. Use your own responses with *then* or *in that case*.

3 Strategies

A Circle the best options to complete the rest of Carmen and Tara's conversation. Sometimes both are correct. Then practice in pairs.

Carmen: So if there are hundreds of people on the site, how do you choose one, **then / in a word**?

Tara: Well, you fill out a long questionnaire about yourself and the site gives you a short list. **In that case / At the end of the day,** they do all the hard work and match potential dates.

Carmen: So **in that case / in a word,** the computer chooses someone?

Tara: No. Well, kind of. I mean, it gives you a selection to choose from based on your questionnaire. I mean, **in that case / when all's said and done,** it's pretty efficient.

Carmen: That's one way of putting it. But I suppose it's just like regular dating. I guess **in the end / in that case**, it's really no different from meeting a stranger at a party.

About you | **B** Pair work What are the best ways to meet people? Discuss the ideas below and add your own.

online dating   through friends   at work / school   through parents   at clubs

Lesson D Smart families

1 Reading

A Prepare Look at the title of the article and the photo. Brainstorm ideas, words, and expressions that you expect the writer to include. What arguments do you expect to read?

B  Read for main ideas Read the article. How many of your ideas were included?

TECHNOLOGY –
is it driving families apart?

1 Look inside any family home in the evening, and you might see a typical enough scene: Mom and Dad, each on their own laptop or tablet, streaming movies, catching up on work, or maybe answering email on their smartphones. Meanwhile, one child is chatting online with one school friend while texting another. The other is playing a video game with a friend on the other side of the city at the same time as playing chess against an uncle in another state. Each member of the family is totally absorbed in his or her own piece of technology. How you interpret such a scene might depend on your attitude toward technology. Do you see a close family that is enjoying "quality time" together? Or do you perceive this family unit as "together" only in a physical sense, as a dysfunctional family whose members are isolated from one another, inhabiting parallel virtual worlds?

2 For some, the effect of technology on human relationships is worrisome. It appears to be the case that many people would much rather spend time with their gadgets than with one another. Technology, they claim, becomes a substitute for face-to-face human relationships, which is a cause for concern.

3 According to some experts, technology is changing how people interact with each another, and for the worse. Some teachers say it is difficult to get students' attention and they have to compete with texting and surfing the Web to such an extent that many schools now require students to leave mobile devices in their lockers. In the same way, young people try to get their parents' attention but have to contend with smartphones, tablets, and other technology.

4 However, a report from the Pew Internet and American Life Project offers a more hopeful and encouraging view, suggesting that far from replacing human contact, new technology can actually enhance family relationships. Just over half of the 2,253 people surveyed agreed that technology had enabled them to increase their contact with distant family members and 47 percent said it had improved the interactions with the people they live with.

5 Thanks to more sophisticated, lighter, and more portable tablet, smartphone, and computer technology, family members who might otherwise have sat in separate rooms can now be in the same one while still occupying a different mental space. Look back at our typical family scene above. Is it any different from four people reading their own books? Does the fact that each person is immersed in a screen rather than a paper page make their activity any less sociable?

6 Moreover, even the closest of families and couples need time away from each other at some point to pursue their own interests. Technology allows people to be both present and absent simultaneously.

7 Where technology will lead us remains to be seen. How it affects the quality of our family relationships is up to all of us.

Reading tip
Writers sometimes give their own views in a question. *Is it any different from four people reading their own books?*

C Read for inference Do you think the writer would answer "yes" or "no" to these questions? Give reasons for your answers.

- Is technology driving families apart?
- Is reading books better for family relationships?
- Should families spend as much of their free time together as possible?
- Do we know where technology will lead us?
- Is it the responsibility of families to decide what impact technology has on their relationships?

D Read for detail Are the sentences true (T), false (F), or is the information not given (NG)? Find evidence in the article for your answers. Then compare with a partner.

1. The writer believes the family in the example is dysfunctional. _____
2. Some people believe that we prefer the company of our computers to being with other people. _____
3. Teachers who can't get their students' attention resort to using technology. _____
4. The Pew study says that technology makes family relationships more distant. _____
5. Technology allows people to do their own thing in the same part of the house. _____
6. Reading is better for family life than using computers. _____

2 Focus on vocabulary Building synonyms

A Replace the words in bold with expressions from the article. You may have to change the form.

1. When you read the first paragraph, how did you **understand** the family scene? (para. 1)
   Did you **see a family that doesn't get along**? (2 expressions, para. 1)
2. Do you think technology is **replacing** face-to-face relationships? (para. 2)
   Is this **something that you worry about**? (2 expressions, para. 2)
3. When have you had to **compete** with technology to get someone's attention? (para. 3)
4. Can technology **improve** family relationships, in your opinion? (para. 4)
5. Is it rude to be **absorbed** in a screen when you are with other people? (para. 5)
6. How often do you use more than one piece of technology **at the same time**? (para. 6)
7. Do you think it's important for families to **do** different activities? Why? Why not? (para. 6)

About you

B Pair work Ask and answer the questions above. Use all the new expressions in your answers.

3 Listening and speaking Keeping tabs on the family

A 🔊 CD 3.09 Look at the ways of monitoring people. Which family members might use them and why? Then listen to a radio show and check (✓) the devices the expert describes.

	Who might use it?	What does it do?
☐ parental controls on a computer		
☐ a screen-time control device		
☐ a GPS tracking device for the car		
☐ a camera in the living room		
☐ a device that detects body movement		

B 🔊 CD 3.10 Listen again and answer the questions in the chart. Write one example for each item.

About you

C Pair work Do you agree with the expert's views? What do you think about each monitoring device in the chart? Would you ever use one? How would you feel if someone monitored you?

Unit 7: Relationships 81

Writing *It just takes a little thought.*

In this lesson, you . . .
- write a magazine article.
- use expressions like *a number of* and *a little*.
- avoid errors with *a number of*, etc.

Task Write a magazine article.
A college magazine has asked you to write an article called *Enhancing friendships – a how-to guide*.

A **Look at a model** Look at the extract from an article. Which topics does it cover? Write them in the article. Brainstorm other ideas that the article could include.

> being considerate   communication   remembering birthdays, etc.   spending time together

> Relationships with friends are very important to our well-being. However, many of us often take the people closest to us for granted, which can result in losing friends. There are a number of factors that lead to improved relationships, including _____, _____, and support. With just a little thought, you can enhance any friendship. . . .
>
> There are a variety of ways to keep in touch with people. Social networks, texts, and phone calls enable us to find out what is happening in our friends' lives and update them about events in our own. They don't take a great deal of effort but do contribute to a feeling of closeness.
>
> Not seeing friends can have a negative impact on your relationship. Therefore, it's important to spend a certain amount of time with them.

B **Focus on language** Read the chart. Underline examples of the expressions in the article above.

Expressing number and amount in writing

With plural countable nouns, you can use: *a (large / huge / small) number of, a (wide) variety of, a (wide) range of, several, many, various; a few* (= some), *few* (= not many).
*There are **a number of / several** factors that lead to improved relationships.*

With uncountable nouns, you can use: *a great deal of, a(n) (large / small) amount of; a little* (= some), *little* (= not much).
*They don't take **a great deal of** time / effort. It takes **little** time / **a little** thought.*

Expressing effect
contribute to, create, lead to, result in, affect, have an effect / impact on, as a result, . . .

Common errors
Use a plural verb with *a number of, several*, etc. + plural noun.
*There **are** a number of factors that **lead to** . . .* (NOT *There is . . . that leads to . . .*)

C Circle the best expressions to complete the article. Sometimes there are two.

Spending quality time together doesn't need to cost **a huge amount of / a number of / various** money. It just takes **little / a little / a small amount of** imagination. **Few / A few / A variety of** friendships can survive without regular contact, and there are **various / a great deal of / a variety of** ways you can spend meaningful time together. Here are just **a little / a few / few** ideas: Take a walk. Go to a museum. Exercise.

Sending a message to say "Hi" doesn't take **a great deal of / several / little** time, either, but it can create **a number of / an enormous amount of** goodwill. Don't just send messages on birthdays or other special occasions. A birthday card may have **little / several / a few** effect if you are not in regular contact. You can find **a range of / various / few** websites that have fun greeting cards to send at any time of year.

D **Write and check** Look at the Task at the top of the page. Write your article. Then check for errors.

Unit 7: Relationships

Vocabulary notebook *Now or never*

Learning tip   Personalized sentences

When you learn a new expression, use it in a personalized sentence to help you remember it.

pain and suffering
Divorce can cause a lot of pain and suffering, and I feel lucky that my parents never got divorced.

A   Use the expressions in the box to complete the sentences.

| above and beyond | live and work | success or failure | back and forth | sick and tired | wait and see |

1. I'm not sure how I did on my last exam. I'll just have to _____.
2. People are always throwing trash around in my neighborhood. I'm _____ of it.
3. My dad is so great. If I ever ask a favor, he always goes _____ what I ask for.
4. What determines the _____ of a relationship is your ability to communicate.
5. When I'm working on a project with classmates, we send each other files _____ all day.
6. I'm lucky that I get to _____ in the same city.

B   Write personalized sentences for these expressions.

1. time and energy _____
2. stop and think _____
3. ups and downs _____
4. give-and-take _____
5. sooner or later _____
6. slowly but surely _____

C   **Word builder**   Find the meanings of these expressions. Then use each one in a personalized sentence.

| far and away | now and then | out and about | to and from |
| last but not least | now or never | over and above | |

I think communication is far and away the most important thing in any relationship.

D   **Focus on vocabulary**   Complete the questions with the words in the box. Then write true answers. Refer to Exercise 2A on page 81 to help you.

| contend   dysfunctional   enhance   immersed   perceive   pursue   simultaneously   substitute   worrisome |

1. Why do you think some families are _____? What can _____ their relationships?
2. Is a long email from a friend a good _____ for having a conversation with that person?
3. Do you _____ any differences in the way that older and younger people use technology?
4. Do you find it _____ that people spend so much time on their computers?
5. Do you ever have to _____ with television to get the attention of your family?
6. Do you ever get so _____ in your work that you forget to have dinner?
7. What two things can you do _____?
8. Are there any interests you'd like to _____ when you're older?

Unit 7: Relationships   83

Unit 8 History

In Unit 8, you . . .
- talk about events in history and famous historical figures.
- use the perfect infinitive after verbs like *seem* and *would like*.
- use *it*-cleft sentences to focus on information.
- avoid topics of conversation with expressions like *Let's not go there*.
- say *That's what I'm saying* to focus on your viewpoint.

Lesson A People in history

1 Grammar in context

A Who are the most famous figures in your country's history? Why are they famous?

"Atatürk is probably one of the most famous, being the founder of the Republic of Turkey."

B 🔊 CD 3.11 Listen to four people talk about historical figures they wish they could have met. What reasons do they give?

WHICH HISTORICAL FIGURE WOULD YOU LIKE TO HAVE MET AND WHY?

For me it would definitely be Leonardo da Vinci. I'd love to have met him; he was such a creative genius and not just an artist. He seems to have foreseen a number of inventions that only came about hundreds of years later, like flying machines and types of weapons. I'd like to tell him he really did see the future.
— Naomi, Chicago

I'd choose Cleopatra – the last pharaoh of ancient Egypt. She is thought to have been very beautiful and is generally considered to have formed some extremely effective political alliances. Not many women were that influential in ancient times. I'd like to have seen how she did it.
— Lucinda, Nairobi

I'm Latin American, so I would nominate Simón Bolívar as the person I would like to have known. He's supposed to have been a very charismatic, courageous leader and is acknowledged to have helped achieve independence for several countries in Latin America in the nineteenth century.
— Patricio, Caracas

I studied philosophy, so I would like to have spoken face-to-face with the Chinese philosopher Confucius. I'd like to have discussed with him his political philosophy and his ideas about family values. He seems to have had a lot of respect for older people, and even though he lived more than a thousand years ago, his beliefs are still relevant.
— Li-yun, Shanghai

About you

C **Pair work** Discuss the questions about the people above. Give reasons for your views.

Which figure do you think . . .

1. attracted admiration and gained the most respect?
2. was the most intelligent and the most talented?
3. had ideas that could be applied nowadays?
4. was particularly clever at political relations?
5. accomplished the most?
6. would make the best role model?

2 Grammar Referring to past time

Figure it out

A Use the interviews to help you complete the answers. Then read the grammar chart.

1. What type of leader was Simón Bolívar? He seems _____.
2. Was Cleopatra good at politics? Yes, she is acknowledged _____.
3. Who does Naomi wish she could have met? She'd like _____.

The perfect infinitive

Grammar extra See page 158.

Use the perfect infinitive for events in a period of time that lead up to the present or to a point in the past.
You can use the perfect infinitive after verbs like *seem, appear,* and *happen*.
He seems **to have had** a lot of respect for older people.

You can use the perfect infinitive after verbs such as *acknowledge, believe, consider, know, say,* and *think* when they are in the passive, and after *be supposed to*.
She is considered **to have formed** some extremely effective political alliances.

You can use the perfect infinitive after *would like / love / hate,* etc., for events that did not happen.
I'd love **to have met** Leonardo da Vinci.
Li-yun would like **to have spoken** face-to-face with Confucius.

In conversation . . .
People generally say, e.g., *I would have liked to do it*, not *I would like to have done it*. Some also say, *I would have liked to have done it*.

B Complete the sentences using the verbs given and a perfect infinitive. Some verbs are passive.

What famous person or people would you like to have met?

1. _____ (would love / meet) Mozart. He _____ (seem / be) a brilliant musician, and he _____ (say / start) composing music at the age of five, which is amazing. He _____ (think / die) from some kind of fever.
2. I _____ ('d like / travel) with Neil Armstrong, one of the astronauts that landed on the moon. The moon landing _____ (acknowledge / be) a major event in our history. My father _____ (happen / meet) one of the astronauts.
3. I _____ ('d like / interview) the captain of the *Mary Celeste*. The disappearance of everyone on board _____ (consider / be) one of the strangest mysteries of all time. The entire crew _____ (seem / disappear) from the ship for no reason at all.
4. I _____ ('d love / spend) a day with Catherine the Great of Russia. She became empress after the death of her husband, Peter III, and _____ (acknowledge / help) Russia become a great power. She _____ (seem / be) very intelligent.

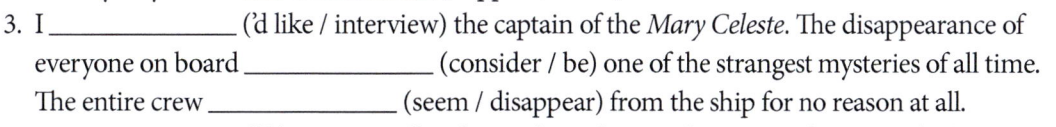

About you

C Pair work Do you agree with the comments above? What would you have asked each person?

3 Viewpoint I'd like to have met . . .

Group work Discuss the questions. Agree on three people that you would all like to have met.

- What famous person from history would you like to have met?
- What contribution is he or she said to have made to history?
- What kind of person is he or she believed to have been?
- What interesting things is he or she supposed to have done?
- What one question would you like to have asked that person?
- How would you like to have spent the day with him or her?

Speaking naturally See page 141.

"I'd love to have met John Lennon. He's generally acknowledged to have been a great songwriter."

Unit 8: History

Lesson B Events that changed the world

1 Vocabulary in context

A What twentieth-century events do you think most changed the world? Make a list.

"I think the invention of the Internet changed the world most. We just can't live without it now."

B CD 3.12 Listen to the podcast. What two broad kinds of historical change are mentioned?

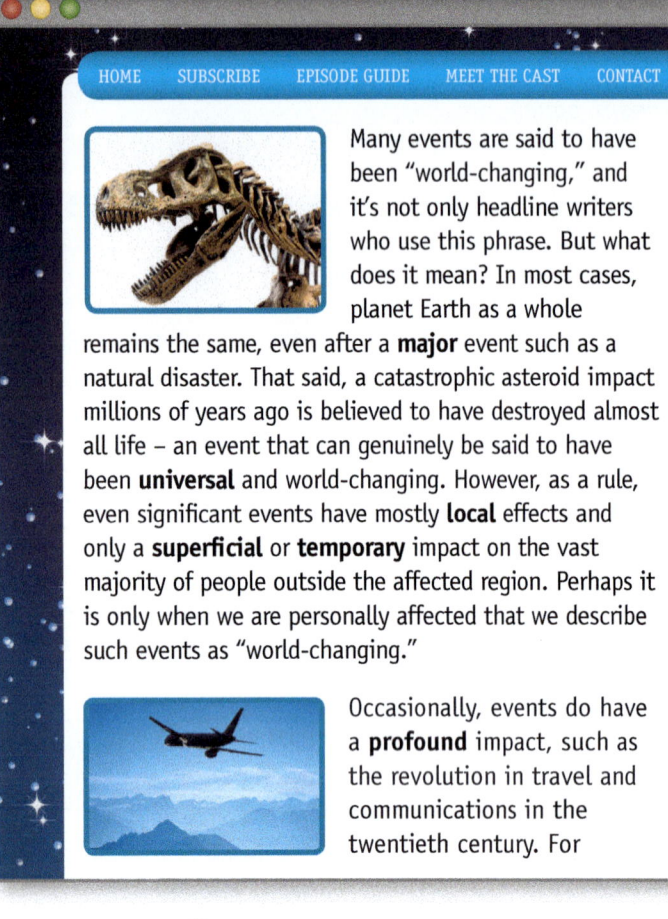

Many events are said to have been "world-changing," and it's not only headline writers who use this phrase. But what does it mean? In most cases, planet Earth as a whole remains the same, even after a **major** event such as a natural disaster. That said, a catastrophic asteroid impact millions of years ago is believed to have destroyed almost all life – an event that can genuinely be said to have been **universal** and world-changing. However, as a rule, even significant events have mostly **local** effects and only a **superficial** or **temporary** impact on the vast majority of people outside the affected region. Perhaps it is only when we are personally affected that we describe such events as "world-changing."

Occasionally, events do have a **profound** impact, such as the revolution in travel and communications in the twentieth century. For example, it was the invention of the airplane that made it possible to cross continents in a matter of hours, and it was when Internet use became widespread that the world turned into a global village. These innovations brought about **massive** changes, and many would now consider it impossible to live without them.

Equally, change can also be **gradual** or **imperceptible**. It was more than 30 years ago that scientists started alerting us to the fact that the world climate was changing, but the change was neither immediately **apparent** nor **sudden**. Events that may seem **minor** or **insignificant** – for example, **slight** or **minute** changes in average global temperatures over a number of years – can make it difficult to predict **lasting** or **long-term** effects. Generally, it is not the small things that we worry about. We react to **visible** or **rapid** change, and it is the events with **immediate** effects that get the headlines.

C Pair work Answer the questions about the podcast.

1. Why does the speaker mention an asteroid strike?
2. What do the airplane and the Internet have in common, from the writer's viewpoint?
3. Why is climate change a different kind of event from the invention of the Internet?

Word sort

D Find adjectives in the podcast that are the opposite of the adjectives below. Can you think of an example of each type of change, effect, or impact?

lasting effects	temporary	**massive** changes	or
significant events		**gradual** change	or
local effects		**imperceptible** change	or
superficial impact			
major event		**long-term** effects	

"The oil spills in the Gulf of Mexico had lasting effects on the tourist industries."

See page 93.

2 Grammar Giving ideas extra focus

Figure it out

A How are these ideas expressed in the podcast? Write sentences. Then read the grammar chart.

1. The invention of the airplane made it possible to cross continents.
2. Headline writers aren't the only ones who use this phrase.
3. The world turned into a global village when Internet use became widespread.

Cleft sentences

Grammar extra See page 159.

You can give extra focus to a single noun, phrase, or clause by putting it at the beginning of the sentence, after *it + be*. After nouns, use a relative pronoun – usually *who* or *that*. After other items, use a *that* clause.

Noun **Scientists** started alerting us to the fact that the world climate was changing.
→ It was **scientists who / that** started alerting us to the fact that the world climate was changing.

Phrase Generally, we don't worry about **the small things**.
→ Generally, it is **not the small things that** we worry about.

Clause We describe events as "world-changing" **only when we are personally affected**.
→ It is **only when we are personally affected that** we describe events as "world-changing."

B Rewrite the numbered sentences as cleft sentences with *it + be* to give extra focus to the underlined words. Then practice telling the information to a partner.

Writing vs. Conversation

It-cleft sentences are about eight times more common in writing.

A. (1) The Internet is a global phenomenon, but a British scientist working in a physics lab in Geneva, Switzerland, invented it. (2) Perhaps the Internet has changed the way people communicate today more than anything else. Tim Berners-Lee devised a new way for scientists to share data by linking documents over the Internet. (3) He took it to the masses only after his bosses rejected his proposal. (4) He posted his idea to an online bulletin board as the "WWW project" at 2:56:20 p.m. on August 6, 1991. (5) He succeeded in creating the World Wide Web because he persisted with his idea. (6) This universal revolution brought us search engines and websites.

B. (1) Two scientists, Francis Crick and James Watson, published an article on April 25, 1953, which answered an age-old question. They had discovered the nature of DNA. (2) This discovery enabled us to understand how parents pass on characteristics, like eye and hair color, to their children. (3) Significant advances in medicine have been possible thanks to their work. In addition, the discovery allowed for the development of criminal forensics. (4) However, DNA wasn't used to convict someone in a criminal case until 1987 in Florida, USA.

About you

C **Pair work** Think of six people or events that have had the most profound effect on our lives. Make a list. Then compare ideas with another pair. Justify your choices.

"We chose the discovery of penicillin because it was penicillin that changed medicine and led to the discovery of other antibiotics."

Unit 8: History 87

Lesson C *Don't get me started.*

1 Conversation strategy Avoiding a topic

A Are you interested in history? Why? Why not? Share your ideas with the class.

B 🔊 CD 3.13 Listen. What does Tom think about history? How about Celia?

Tom You know, I never did like history in school. It just wasn't a subject I enjoyed, remembering all those dates. I didn't see the point.

Celia Well, I guess it's not just about learning dates. It's about trying to understand why people did things or what society was like through the ages.

Tom But I mean, so often the facts get distorted, like what happened in the last war. But don't get me started on that.

Celia Well, yeah. But that doesn't mean we shouldn't try to find out the truth and then learn from it so we don't repeat the same mistakes.

Tom But that's what I'm saying. We don't learn, do we? I mean, look at what's happening around the world today. We seem to have learned absolutely nothing. It's like history repeating itself. But that's another story.

Celia Yeah, but even if we still have disputes, maybe we'll deal with them in a different way. I mean, engage in dialog . . . negotiate.

Tom But most of the time, talks just break down and don't go anywhere. But anyway, let's not get into politics.

C **Notice** how Tom uses expressions like these to avoid talking about certain topics. Find examples in the conversation.

> Don't get me started (on . . .).
> (But) that's another / a whole other story.
> Let's not go there.
> Let's not get into / talk about politics / that.
> I'd rather not talk about it / that.

In conversation . . .

People say *Don't get me started* about a topic they find annoying, and often before they say more about it. *I'd rather not talk about it* is a more serious way to show you want to avoid a topic.

D 🔊 CD 3.14 Listen to more of the conversation. Complete the expressions that you hear. Then practice the whole conversation with a partner.

Celia I know. There've been some terrible events in recent history, as you know.

Tom I know, _____. We probably won't agree on anything, so _____.

Celia OK, but it's amazing how little people know of their own country's history _____.

Tom Yeah, but there'll always be different versions of events, like the latest peace talks. _____.

Celia Yeah. They seem to have collapsed. _____. You know, I wonder how future generations will see us.

Tom Greedy and aggressive, I'd say. You know what I think. _____.

Unit 8: History

2 Strategy plus *That's what I'm saying.*

🔊 **CD 3.15** You can use **That's what I'm saying** in responses to focus on your viewpoint.

> But **that's what I'm saying**. We don't learn, do we?

In conversation . . .
People also say *That's what I mean / meant.*

🔊 **CD 3.16** **Complete each conversation with two responses from the box. Write a–f. Then listen and practice. Practice again, this time giving your own answers to the questions.**

a. That's what I meant. There's something in it for everyone.
b. Yeah. That's what I'm saying. You need to know the context.
c. That's what I'm saying. And literacy is an important part of that. And now, of course, there's the Internet.
d. That's what I'm saying. It's such a broad area that it includes anything and everything.
e. Exactly. That's what I mean. You need to know how it's developed to interpret it.
f. Right. That's what I'm saying. Beliefs, opinions, philosophy – they all shape our actions.

1. *A* History is an interesting area because you can study the history of anything, can't you?
   B I suppose it involves everything from everyday life to great political events and wars and so on.
   A ☐ ☐

2. *A* Do you think you need to know the history of art to appreciate it?
   B Well, all art builds on the past, either by developing or rejecting it.
   A ☐ ☐

3. *A* I guess I'm interested in the history of ideas, like how ideas spread. Isn't that what's important?
   B Yeah. I guess new ideas help us develop and keep history moving.
   A ☐ ☐

3 Listening and strategies *Tracing family histories*

A 🔊 **CD 3.17** **Listen to two friends talk about family histories. Complete the sentences. Circle a or b.**

1. Jennifer's great-grandmother was   a) reluctant to emigrate.   b) 80 when she emigrated.
2. Jennifer's great-grandfather   a) was a baker by profession.   b) enjoyed baking as a hobby.
3. She found out her family history   a) from the Internet.   b) from papers in the attic.
4. Patrick would like to have known   a) who his biological mother was.   b) what his original last name was.
5. He says states should help   a) parents raise adopted children.   b) children find their birth family.

B 🔊 **CD 3.18** **Listen again. Answer the questions.**

1. What fact does Patrick mention when he says, "But that's another story"?
2. When Patrick says, "That's what I mean," what is he talking about?
3. Patrick says, "Let's not get into that." What doesn't he want to talk about?

About you

C **Pair work** Discuss the questions.

1. Is it important for people to know about their family history? Why? Why not?
2. Have you or any of your friends tried to trace your family history? Was it successful?
3. What do you know of your family history? Are there any interesting stories?
4. Do you think adopted children should be able to contact their biological family? Why? Why not?

Unit 8: History

Lesson D *Unearthing the past*

1 Reading

A Prepare You are going to read an article about ancient texts. Match the terms on the left with their definitions on the right. Then compare answers with a partner.

1. archaeology _____
2. papyrus _____
3. anthropology _____
4. manuscript _____
5. paleography _____

a. the study and interpretation of ancient writing
b. a document written by hand rather than printed
c. a kind of paper made from a plant that was common in Ancient Egypt
d. the study of human societies based on material evidence left behind
e. the study of human societies and cultures and how they develop

B  **Read for main ideas** Read the article. What is the Ancient Lives Project? How does it work?

THE ANCIENT LIVES PROJECT

1 They may not have had computers, databases, social networking sites, or spreadsheets, but the ancient Egyptians are known to have kept careful written records, not only of important people and events but also of the minute details of everyday life. In 1896–1897, hundreds of thousands of fragments of papyrus with writing on them were found on the edge of a ruined Egyptian city, in a place which is believed to have been the city's landfill. The fragments, which filled 700 boxes, were taken back to Oxford, England. The manuscripts, written in ancient Greek, now belong to the Egypt Exploration Society – an organization that was established over 125 years ago to carry out archaeological fieldwork and research in Egypt.

2 As a rule, it is archaeologists, anthropologists, and paleographers who sift the evidence of our distant past, feed our hunger for knowledge about our ancestors, bring to life dead languages, and paint a detailed picture of ancient life for us. However, in this case, there were simply not enough experts to read all those tantalizing fragments of ancient Greek, so they mostly remained undisturbed in their boxes. Those pieces that the experts did decipher revealed a fascinating picture of ancient Egyptian life: Literary, religious, and philosophical texts sat alongside bits of gossip, receipts, marriage certificates, personal letters, love potions, wills, sports reports, and other everyday texts.

3 It is not uncommon for archaeologists to involve non-specialists in their work. The two men who discovered the papyrus fragments hired local labor in Egypt. Every year, volunteers take part in archaeological digs, spending hours on their hands and knees, delicately scraping in the sand and soil of lost cities or the remains of our ancestors' homes. It is this slow, painstaking work that helps archaeologists piece together the jigsaw puzzle of the past. It can also be fun: Working with a team at an archaeological site is how many young people choose to spend their vacations.

4 In 2011, a groundbreaking project was rolled out that allowed volunteers all over the world to help reveal the past while sitting at home in front of a computer screen. The Ancient Lives Project grew from a simple idea – log in at its website, look at a papyrus fragment on your screen, check each symbol you see against an on-screen keyboard of ancient Greek letters, click when you think you have a match, and after a few minutes' work, upload the results to the project's paleographers. It is this imaginative use of the collective labor of thousands of volunteers and "armchair archaeologists" that now enables the experts to read and share with us the hundreds of thousands of manuscripts so that we can look into a window on the past. And who knows? We may even see our own reflection.

Reading tip
Writers sometimes use a pronoun in a way that means you have to read on to find out what it means, as with the first word of the article *(They . . .)*.

90 Unit 8: History

About you

C **Check your understanding** Are the statements true (T) or false (F) based on the article?

1. The papyrus fragments had been carefully stored away by the Egyptians. ____
2. For a long time, nobody read most of the manuscripts that were found. ____
3. The manuscript fragments were largely official documents. ____
4. Archaeologists often get non-professionals to help with physical work. ____
5. You can earn money by taking part in the Ancient Lives Project. ____
6. You need to be able to understand ancient Greek to participate. ____

About you

D **React** **Pair work** What would the documents you throw away or delete each week reveal to future generations about life today? Discuss.

2 Focus on vocabulary Metaphors

A Find metaphors in the article to replace the words in bold.

1. Archaeologists **work carefully through** the evidence of our distant past. (para. 2) sift
2. Paleographers **translate languages that no one speaks anymore**. (para. 2)
3. Archaeologists **satisfy our desire** for knowledge about our ancestors. (para. 2)
4. They **describe in detail** ancient life. (para. 2)
5. Religious and philosophical texts **were found** alongside bits of gossip, receipts, etc. (para. 2)
6. Volunteers help archaeologists to **build a detailed picture** of the past. (para. 3)
7. In 2011, a project **began** that allowed volunteers to help decipher the manuscripts. (para. 4)
8. The translations of the manuscripts will allow people to **observe** the past. (para. 4)

B **Pair work** How important is it to "unearth the past"? Discuss, using the metaphors above.

3 Listening Citizen participation projects

A CD 3.19 Listen to a talk about citizen participation projects. Check (✓) the ones described.

☐ 1. Ships' records ☐ 2. Whales communicating ☐ 3. Visible stars ☐ 4. The language of apes ☐ 5. The surface of the moon

B CD 3.20 Listen again. Complete each sentence with three words.

1. The work of volunteers has made _____ to the Ancient Lives Project.
2. The volunteers who sit at their computers doing this kind of work are _____.
3. A project that would have taken 28 years can be done in _____ months with the help of citizen volunteers.
4. In the Old Weather Project, people are looking at _____ from World War I.
5. The data from the Old Weather Project will be used to predict _____.
6. Discovering stories from these ships is also _____.

About you

C **Pair work** Which projects seem most interesting? Would you like to take part in one?

Unit 8: History 91

Writing *In the end, . . .*

In this lesson, you . . .
- write a narrative essay.
- order events in the past.
- avoid errors with *in the end* and *at the end*.

Task Write a historical narrative.
You have been asked to write a history of your family, a family member, or someone in the community for a website. Write a short essay.

A Look at a model Look at the extracts from a narrative essay. Order the events 1–4.

☐ Annie left her hometown.   ☐ Annie got married.   ☐ The war started.   ☐ Annie's parents died.

> My mother, Annie Mason, left the city where she lived shortly after the war started and went to work on a farm in the country. Prior to leaving home, she had lost both her parents in the war. Shocked and saddened by this tragedy, she decided to leave the city. As the train took her away from her old life, she felt sad and lonely. . . .
>
> On arriving at the country station, she met a young man who offered to carry her bags. This was the man who eventually became my father. It was love at first sight. Finally, she had a chance of happiness.
>
> They moved back to the city once the war had ended. As soon as they found jobs, they married and subsequently had four children, all of whom were successful. In the end, they retired to a small house near the railroad station where they'd first met. . . .

B Focus on language Read the chart. Then underline examples of ordering events in Exercise A.

Ordering events in writing

You can use these structures to vary the way you present the order of events.

Time clauses	**After / Once / As soon as** the war ended, they married. **On arriving at the station,** she met my father.
Participle clauses	**Arriving at the station,** she met my father. **Saddened by this tragedy,** she decided to leave the city.
Adverbs and adverbial phrases	She had **previously** lived in the city. They **subsequently / eventually** had four children. **In the end, / After a while,** they married.

Writing vs. Conversation
Prepositions + *-ing* are more common in writing.

■ Conversation
■ Writing

C Rewrite these sentences, using the word(s) given and making any other changes.

1. My father met my mother, and then he applied for a job in California. (after)
2. He had lived in the U.S., but he moved back to Mexico when his contract came to an end. (previously)
3. He arrived back in his hometown and met the woman who became my mother. (as soon as / eventually)
4. After they were married, they moved to San Diego. (once)
5. My mother found out that she was pregnant before their fifth wedding anniversary. (prior to)
6. They had three more children and were happy living in the U.S. (after a while)
7. They moved back to Mexico and left their "American life" behind them. (in the end / participle clause)
8. When he walked into his new home, my father vowed he would never leave again. (on)

D Write and check Now write a short essay as described in the Task above. Then check for errors.

Common errors

Use *at the end of* + a noun. **At the end of the war,** they got married.
In the end refers to the conclusion of all the events. **In the end,** they retired.
Use *finally* at the end of a series of other events. She **finally** found happiness.

Unit 8: History

Vocabulary notebook *Deep, low, high*

Learning tip — Synonyms and antonyms

When you learn a new word, look up its synonyms (words with similar meanings) and antonyms (words with opposite meanings). Be careful: Different meanings of a word can have different synonyms and antonyms.

a deep conversation = meaningful, profound
≠ trivial, light-hearted
a deep voice = a low voice
≠ a high-pitched voice

A Underline three antonyms to the words in bold below. Circle the synonym.

1. **significant**   meaningless   insignificant   considerable   unimportant
2. **local**   universal   global   foreign   nearby
3. **superficial**   detailed   meaningless   profound   thorough
4. **imperceptible** unseen   conspicuous   striking   apparent
5. **lasting**   permanent   temporary   brief   fleeting

B Write a synonym and an antonym for each of these words.

	Synonym	Antonym
1. major	_____	_____
2. gradual	_____	_____
3. long-term	_____	_____
4. massive	_____	_____

C **Word builder** These words are all antonyms of words in Exercises A and B. Find their meanings and add them to the examples above.

| abrupt | deep | miniature | obvious | transient |

D **Focus on vocabulary** Match the metaphors from the article on page 91 with their meanings.

Metaphor
1. bring something to life _____
2. sift (through), e.g., evidence, facts _____
3. feed a hunger for knowledge _____
4. paint a detailed picture _____
5. sit alongside _____
6. piece together a jigsaw puzzle of something _____
7. roll out (a project) _____
8. look into a window on _____

Meaning
a. satisfy the desire to learn
b. make something interesting or current
c. observe
d. work carefully through
e. explain or describe in detail
f. begin or put into practice
g. figure out a mystery or problem
h. be (together) with

E Now look at these metaphors. Write the metaphor from Exercise D that means the opposite of each.

1. wind something down *roll out* _____
2. starve someone of something _____
3. kill an idea _____
4. look into a crystal ball _____
5. brush over something _____

Unit 8: History 93

Unit 9

Engineering wonders

In Unit 9, you . . .

- talk about engineering feats, challenges, and developments.
- use *whoever, whatever,* etc., to talk about unknown people or things.
- start sentences with negative adverbs for extra emphasis.
- give facts using expressions like *considering* and *given* (*that*).
- use *at all* and *whatsoever* to emphasize negative ideas.

Lesson A *Engineers change the world.*

1 Grammar in context

A 🔊 CD 3.21 Do you know what engineers do? Make a list. Then read the college web page and see how many of your ideas are mentioned.

Change the world – be an engineer!

Wherever you look, you'll see the work of a talented engineer who has designed, tested, and improved the objects around you. Whatever goes wrong or whenever there is a problem to be solved, however complex, one can rely on engineers to apply their knowledge of math and science – along with some creativity – to come up with a solution. So, what do engineers do? Here's just a sample of their work.

CHEMICAL ENGINEERS Whenever you wash your jeans, remember it was a chemical engineer that developed the fade-resistant dye. Pick up any game console – that scratchproof plastic was made by these engineers. Chemical engineers also help produce medicines and cosmetics, and find solutions to damage caused by harmful chemicals.

CIVIL ENGINEERS These engineers are at the heart of urban planning and transportation design. Wherever you go and whatever you do today, you'll encounter their work. The system of pipes that brings water to your shower, the roads you drive on, the bridges you cross, the buildings you occupy – these are all examples of civil engineering work.

MATERIALS SCIENCE ENGINEERS Engineers in this field work with materials such as ceramics, plastics, and metals. Their work is central to engineering as a whole. Materials science engineers process, design, and test whatever materials are used in all other branches of engineering.

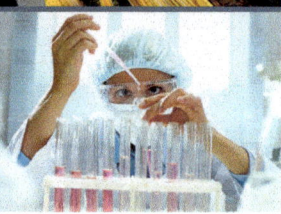

BIOMEDICAL ENGINEERS Bringing together the fields of engineering and medicine, biomedical engineers work on whatever needs to be done to improve health care. They design anything from artificial body parts and lifesaving equipment to drug and gene therapies.

However you look at it, a career in engineering is exciting and rewarding. Whoever you are and whichever field of engineering you choose, you have the potential to design and develop products that will have an enormous impact on society.

B Pair work Discuss the questions.

1. What skills do engineers need, according to the web page?
2. What types of activities do the different fields have in common?
3. Which field of engineering sounds most interesting? Which is most valuable to society?
4. Does the web page succeed in getting people to consider engineering as a career, in your view?

2 Grammar Talking about unknown people and things

Figure it out

A How does the web page express these ideas? Write the phrases. Then read the grammar chart.

1. It doesn't matter what goes wrong. . . .
2. At any time at all when there is a problem to be solved . . .
3. It doesn't matter how you look at it. . . .

whatever, whichever, whoever, whenever, wherever, however

Grammar extra See page 160.

The *-ever* words have the meaning "any at all" or "it doesn't matter what, who, where, etc."

Whatever, whichever can be determiners or pronouns.	**Whatever** goes wrong, one can turn to an engineer. These engineers work on **whatever** (task) needs to be done. **Whichever** (field) you choose, you will make an impact.
Whoever is a pronoun.	**Whoever** you are, you have the potential to impact society.
Whenever, wherever, however are adverbs.	**Whenever** there is a problem, an engineer will fix it. **Wherever** you look, you'll see the work of an engineer. **However** you look at it, a career in engineering is exciting.

In conversation . . .

Whatever is the most frequent. It is often used in the vague expressions *or / and whatever*.
We're not all cut out to be engineers **or whatever**.

B 🔊 CD 3.22 Complete the sentences with *-ever* words. Then listen and check.

1. **A** Do you really understand what engineers do?
   B Well, I didn't until now. I mean, _____ someone said they were studying engineering, I never really understood what they were doing.
   C I do – well, kind of. My friend's an electrical engineer, and he told me that _____ I use like a cell phone or satellite TV or _____, that's the kind of thing he's worked on.

2. **A** Do you have what it takes to be an engineer?
   B Sure. _____ there's a problem at home, I can usually fix it.
   C Me? Absolutely not. _____ way I look at it, I'm not cut out to be an engineer.

3. **A** Do you think engineering could be an exciting career?
   B Oh, definitely. _____ says it's boring doesn't know what they're talking about. I mean, _____ field of engineering you look at, there's something interesting.
   C It depends. I mean, designing things for space stations or _____ sounds fun.

4. **A** Do you ever think about how roads and bridges and _____ actually get built?
   B Yes. _____ I see a new bridge or skyscraper or _____ being built, I think _____ designed all that must be a genius. It's amazing how it's all planned and managed.
   C Yeah. _____ you think of high-rise buildings, you have to admire _____ built them.

About you

C *Group work* Take turns answering the questions. Who knows the most about engineering? Who would be most suited to a career in engineering?

Unit 9: Engineering wonders 95

Lesson B *Incredible feats*

1 Vocabulary in context

A 🔊 CD 3.23 Read the article. Why was constructing the bridge so challenging?

The Millau Viaduct in southern France has been called "the freeway in the sky." On stormy days, it looks as though it is floating above the clouds. No wonder. When constructed, it was the world's tallest road bridge at 343 meters (1,125 feet) at its highest point above the River Tarn. Never before had engineers attempted to build a bridge of this size and scale. At the outset, little did they realize how much the project would push the boundaries of engineering to its limits. Nor did they know how many problems they would face. However, not once did the engineers fail to find a solution.

The viaduct is a four-lane highway across one of the deepest valleys in France. Not only does it ease the congestion of the north–south routed traffic between Paris and Spain, but it has become one of the country's most celebrated projects – a landmark in itself.

Engineers faced three challenges in building the viaduct. They had to:

- **construct** the tallest **concrete** bridge piers (supporting towers) in the world;
- **assemble** and **maneuver** a 36,000-tonne (40,000-ton), 2.5-kilometer (1.5-mile) freeway, rolling it out to **position** it onto the top of the towers;
- **erect** seven massive **steel** pylons, each weighing 700 tonnes (770 tons), and **install** 11 pairs of steel cables.

In addition, not only did this dangerous work have to be done way above the ground at a height taller than the Eiffel Tower, but it had to be completed in four years! Nowhere else on Earth had engineers accomplished a project of this magnitude **in such a short time frame**. By comparison, one of the longest bridges in the world – the Akashi-Kaikyo in Japan – took 10 years to complete. However, under no circumstances could the project **fall behind schedule**. Any **delays** would have cost the construction company $30,000 a day in penalties. Not only did they **complete** it **on time**, but the viaduct opened a month **ahead of schedule**.

The biggest challenge of all, apart from **engineering** the bridge to be strong enough to withstand the elements, was to make it blend into the beautiful landscape. Only by **elevating** the highway so far above ground and slimming down the towers and road deck were the architects able to achieve such a delicate and stunning visual impact.   [more]

Word sort

B Complete the chart with vocabulary in the article. Add other items you want to learn. Then tell a partner about engineering feats you know of.

materials	build	move	schedules	other
	construct			

"Well, one that comes to mind is the airport they constructed in Hong Kong. They built an island to put it on."

See page 103.

2 Grammar Emphasizing ideas

Figure it out

A Underline the sentences in the article that express the same ideas as the sentences below. Then read the grammar chart.

1. They not only completed it on time, but the viaduct opened a month ahead of schedule.
2. Engineers had never before attempted to build a bridge of this size and scale.
3. They didn't realize how much the project would push the boundaries of engineering.

Negative adverbs and word order

Grammar extra See page 161.

If you use a negative adverb (e.g., *never, not*) to start a sentence for emphasis, put the verb before the **subject**. Use *do* or *does* for simple present and *did* for simple past verbs.
Not only **does it ease** traffic congestion, but it has become a landmark.
Not once **did the engineers fail** to find a solution.
Never before **had engineers attempted** to build a bridge like this.

Use the same inversion after *little*, *rarely*, and *only* + prepositional phrase.
Only by elevating the highway **were the architects** able to achieve the stunning visual impact.

Writing vs. Conversation
The inverted forms are about three times more common in formal writing than in conversation.

B CD 3.24 Rewrite the sentences starting with the words given. Make any other necessary changes. Listen and check. Then close your book. How much information can you remember?

1. They not only had to erect seven towers taller than the Eiffel Tower, but they also had to make sure the towers were at exactly the right point. *Not only . . .*
2. They supplied the concrete by building a concrete factory on-site. *Only . . .*
3. Engineers have rarely constructed freeways out of steel. *Rarely . . .*
4. Engineers had never before built such a tall bridge. *Never before . . .*
5. No one had positioned a road onto towers in this way. *Nor . . .*
6. They didn't realize how difficult it would be. *Little . . .*
7. You never hear of projects like this going according to schedule. *Never . . .*

3 Listening Other amazing feats

A CD 3.25 Listen to three extracts from a documentary. What project is being described? Number the pictures 1–3. There is one extra.

☐ the Queen Mary 2

☐ Palm Islands, Dubai

☐ Churaumi Aquarium, Japan

☐ Channel Tunnel, Britain / France

B CD 3.26 Listen again. Answer the questions about each project.

1. What was the main challenge of the project?
2. What specific aims were engineers trying to accomplish?
3. What world record did it break at the time?
4. How many people use the facility annually?

C Pair work Choose an engineering feat from the lesson or another you know about. Prepare a presentation to give to the class.

Unit 9: Engineering wonders   97

Lesson C *It makes no sense whatsoever.*

1 Conversation strategy Supporting ideas

A What are the biggest challenges engineers will face in the next century? Make a list.

Not only will there be more people, but there'll be more cars. So building roads will be a challenge.

B 🔊 CD 3.27 Listen. What challenges do Sonia and Scott talk about?

Sonia I was just listening to a report on the radio about engineering challenges for the next century.

Scott Yeah? Let me guess. Is one of them building a colony on Mars? I mean, it makes no sense whatsoever, but . . .

Sonia No, and in view of the fact that it takes about seven months to get there, that's a long way off.

Scott Right. OK. Well, let's see, um, considering the price of gas, maybe finding cheaper sources of fuel?

Sonia Yeah, there were a couple about energy – like making solar energy economical. But there's one that's kind of surprising, given the weather.

Scott Uh-huh. Yeah?

Sonia Providing access to clean water.

Scott Oh, right. That's pretty basic considering we're in the twenty-first century. But I guess it makes sense in light of the fact that some places got no rain at all last year. I mean, none whatsoever.

Sonia Yeah, they were saying one in six people don't have access to clean water for whatever reason.

C **Notice** how Sonia and Scott use facts to support their opinions and thoughts, using expressions like these. Find the examples in the conversation.

> considering
> given (that / the fact that)
> in view of / in light of (the fact that)

D 🔊 CD 3.28 Listen. Complete the sentences with the expressions you hear.

1. _____ the world's population is growing, I predict there'll be a crisis over water one day.
2. For some regions, access to water should be relatively easy, _____ the technology to extract water from underground already exists.
3. Having clean water is a really pressing problem, especially _____ something like 80 percent of illnesses in developing countries are linked to poor water conditions.
4. _____ over 90 percent of the world's water is in the ocean, we should find a way to use more sea water for drinking water.
5. _____ everyone needs water, you'd think more people would be concerned about it.
6. _____ how precious clean water is, we should pay more for it and people should be fined if they waste it.

About you

E **Pair work** Discuss the statements in Exercise D. What are your views?

A *I think there will definitely be a crisis over water supplies in the future.*
B *Especially considering it's such a basic need. Some people say it will even lead to conflicts.*

Unit 9: Engineering wonders

2 Strategy plus *at all, whatsoever*

◆)) CD 3.29 You can use **at all** or **whatsoever** to emphasize a negative phrase.

Whatsoever is more emphatic. It is mostly used after **no . . .**, **not any . . .**, or **none**.

Some places got **no** rain **at all**. I mean, **none whatsoever**.

In conversation . . .

Whatsoever is typically used after *none, nothing,* or these nouns: *(no / any) problem(s), reason, sense, evidence, doubt(s), impact, effect.*

About you | **Find two responses for each comment. Write the letters a–f. Then practice in pairs. Continue the conversations.**

1. Engineering is so important, yet it's not a subject you can take in high school. ____ ____
2. It seems that either money or politics gets in the way of finding solutions to most problems. ____ ____
3. It takes years before engineering breakthroughs affect most people's lives. ____ ____

a. Right. But there's no doubt whatsoever that we can solve these issues.
b. Yes, a lot of them have no impact on us whatsoever.
c. Right. It makes no sense whatsoever. I mean, we should just get on with it and sort these things out.
d. I know. There are no classes in it at all. There was nothing whatsoever like that when I was a kid.
e. Well, I don't see much evidence at all for that. It depends what advances you mean.
f. Yeah, and there shouldn't be any problem at all including it in the curriculum.

3 Strategies *More priorities*

A Circle the correct options to complete the conversations. Circle both options if they are both correct. Then practice with a partner. Practice again, using different expressions.

1. **A** I wonder what some of the other engineering challenges are. Do you have any ideas?
   B Well, mapping the brain would be a huge breakthrough. I mean, **given / considering** that we know so little about diseases like Alzheimer's.
   A Oh, there's no doubt **whatsoever / in view of the fact that**. If they could treat brain disorders, that would be huge. I mean, they have no cure **whatsoever / at all** for migraines, even.

2. **A** What's the most *immediate* challenge, do you think?
   B Well, they need to update a lot of the infrastructure in many cities. **Considering / In light of** the fact that so many of the subways and sewers are so old, that should be a priority.
   A True. And there's no reason **considering / at all** not to do that now. They know how to.

3. **A** Do you think developing space technology and exploring Mars is a priority?
   B I don't know. I don't think it has any impact **whatsoever / given** on our daily lives. Though I guess studying asteroids might be good, **in view of / given** that we've been hit by asteroids in the past.

About you | **B** **Pair work** Ask and answer the questions in Exercise A. Give your own answers.

Speaking naturally
See page 142.

Unit 9: Engineering wonders 99

Lesson D Robotics

1 Reading

A Prepare What do you know about robots? How are robots used? Make a list. Then scan the article to see if your ideas are mentioned.

Robots are used in the medical field for things like keyhole surgery.

B  **Read for main ideas** Read the article. Then check (✓) the best title for the article.

1. ☐ Robots cause unimaginable problems
2. ☐ The future is here and it's robotic
3. ☐ Home is where your robot is

1 Robots are probably not high on the list of priorities for the average consumer. The nearest they might come to a robot is a robotic vacuum cleaner, which maneuvers its way around the home picking up dust. For most people, not only is the thought of interacting with a humanoid robot in their kitchen highly unlikely, but it also seems a little absurd. Some even consider it positively creepy, which may in part be because people are unsure how to relate to a robot. Such reluctance might also be explained by the ethical dilemmas posed by using robots instead of real people for certain tasks. Is it acceptable, for example, to have robots babysitting our children or looking after our elderly?

2 Robots have of course played a critical part in society for decades. In the 1960s, robots transformed the automotive industry by performing hazardous and repetitive tasks and working more efficiently and more accurately than humans. They could also work longer hours, which undoubtedly had an enormous impact on the profitability of the industry. Since then, industrial robots have been deployed in various manufacturing and electronics industries. Many of the products we purchase have been assembled or handled in some way by robots. Little do consumers realize how much their lives are actually already influenced by robotics.

3 If you consider the robotics industry today, there doesn't seem to be a field that is *not* influenced by robotics in significant ways. Indeed, robotics now plays a role in everything from agriculture and forestry to mining and construction – even to warfare.

Medical robotics
4 For years now, surgeons have been using robots in performing different types of operations. Not only is robotic surgery less invasive, but recovery for the patient is much quicker. More recent groundbreaking developments may have a profound impact on identifying and treating serious diseases. For example, ETH Zürich researchers have developed micro-robots that are the size of bacteria. While more research needs to be conducted, possible applications include carrying medicine to specific areas of the body and treating heart disease.

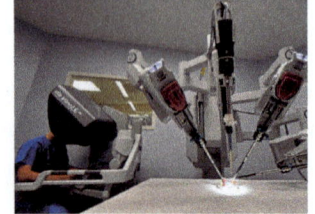

Search and rescue
5 Whatever challenges responders face when they arrive at a large-scale disaster site – for example, after an earthquake – one of the greatest is determining where victims may still be trapped. Germany's Fraunhofer Institute has been developing a robotic "spider" that can easily move through the debris of collapsed buildings and send rescuers live images or even sense hazards such as leaking gas. The advantages of using robots as opposed to humans in these situations are obvious.

Ocean exploration
6 U.S. Navy-backed research has produced a robotic "jellyfish" that can power itself using hydrogen from seawater. Possible applications include monitoring oceans for signs of pollution or for security purposes, and for exploration of otherwise inaccessible ocean waters.

7 However you look at it, robots will increasingly be part of our lives in the future. The field of robotics is rapidly expanding, and scientists are forging ahead with developing robots that can see, speak, think, and even make decisions based on the environment around them. The applications of robotics seem unlimited, and certainly the general public might perceive the advantages of using robots in specialized areas. The question remains: How accepting will we be of having robots rather than humans, as caregivers for our families?

C **Understanding inference** Do the statements below agree with the information in the article? Write Y (Yes), N (No), or NG (Information not given).

1. The average consumer really wants to get a robot for their home. _____
2. It's generally more efficient to use robots in industry. _____
3. Patients who have robotic surgery live longer. _____
4. The robotic spider decides where it should go to find victims of earthquakes. _____
5. The robotic jellyfish can go to places where humans can't normally go. _____
6. Robots will always play a limited part in our lives in the future. _____

2 Focus on vocabulary Verbs

A Find verbs with similar meanings to the verbs in bold. Rewrite the questions, using the correct forms of the verbs and making any other changes needed.

1. Given that robots have no emotions, can we really **communicate** or **connect with** them? (para. 1)
2. If you were to **do** a survey of friends, do you think they would want a robot in their home? (para. 4)
3. Can you **recognize** the ways in which humanoid robots are lacking? (para. 4)
4. What industries do you know of where robots are **used**? What jobs do they **do**? (para. 2)
5. How do you think robots will **change** the workplace in the future? (para. 2)
6. How would you **decide** if robots could make good caregivers or teachers? (para. 5)
7. Will we need to **watch** robots to make sure that they don't become more powerful than humans? (para. 6)

About you

B **Pair work** Discuss the questions above. Think of as many ideas as you can.

3 Listening Is she for real?

A Read the questions about a humanoid robot. Can you guess the answers?

1. ☐ How did they build "her"?
2. ☐ What can "she" do?
3. ☐ How much did she cost to build?
4. ☐ How do people react to her?
5. ☐ What applications does she have?
6. ☐ What are the ethical issues of "human" robots?
7. ☐ Do people want robots as friends?

B 🔊 CD 3.30 Listen to a radio interview. Which questions does the guest answer? Check (✓) the boxes.

C 🔊 CD 3.31 Listen again. Write one detail to answer the questions you checked in Exercise B.

Geminoid F

4 Viewpoint Applications for the future

Group work Imagine there are no technological barriers whatsoever. How could robots be useful? Discuss your ideas about specific applications. What are your top 10 ideas?

"You could have a robot that mows lawns – kind of like a robot vacuum cleaner. The thing is you'd have to make sure it didn't cut down all your flowers."

In conversation . . .
You can use *The thing is . . .* to introduce ideas or problems.

Unit 9: Engineering wonders   101

Writing *A good alternative*

In this lesson, you . . .
- write a classification essay.
- express alternatives.
- avoid errors with *would rather / rather than*.

Task Write an essay.
Can robots replace human beings in all activities? Give reasons and examples in your response.

A Look at a model Look at these extracts from an essay. Think of a topic to add to each paragraph.

. . . There are a number of fields in which robots can and should be used as opposed to human beings. These can be classified into the following types: dangerous activities; tasks requiring extreme precision; tedious, repetitive work; and activities that require huge computing power. One area is in heavy industry, where robots are already used instead of human beings. Not only can they do dangerous or unpleasant jobs, they are also more efficient. Another example of where robots are a good alternative to humans is in space exploration. . . . Yet another is . . .

. . . On the other hand, there are some fields where a robot, however smart, would be no substitute for a human being. One example of this is caring for people in hospitals. Although robots can now perform surgery, human caregivers rather than robots are best at satisfying the psychological needs of patients. In fact, most patients would rather be cared for by a human caregiver than a robot. An additional area is . . .

Classifying
There are a number of . . .
One is . . . Another . . . Yet another . . .
They can be classified into the following types: . . .
They can be divided into four groups / categories. The first is . . .

B Focus on language Read the chart. Then underline the expressions for stating alternatives and preference in the paragraphs in Exercise A.

Stating alternatives and preference in writing
You can use these expressions to write about alternatives.
Robots are used in industry **in place of / instead of / rather than** *humans.*
Human caregivers **as opposed to** *robots are best at caring for patients.*
Robots are a good **alternative to / substitute for** *humans in space.*

Would rather, be preferable to, and *be no substitute for* express preference.
Most people **would rather** *have a human caregiver* **than** *a robot.*
Robots **are no substitute for** *humans in some areas.*

In writing . . .
Rather than joins nouns, verbs, prepositional phrases, adjectives, or adverbs. Notice the verb forms after *rather than*.

Rather than **use / using** *humans for these tasks, we should use robots.*

C Complete the sentences with expressions from the chart. How many correct answers are there?

1. In jobs where conditions are dangerous, robots are the obvious _____ human workers.
2. The construction industry could easily use robotic devices _____ human beings.
3. There are many industrial jobs where robots would be a better _____ humans.
4. Manufacturers _____ use robotic technology because it _____ employing people.
5. _____ using human mechanics, some companies now use robots that repair themselves.
6. In teaching, however, _____ use robots as teachers, we should always employ humans.
7. Robots are _____ people when it comes to jobs such as hotel receptionists.

D Write and check Now write your essay as described in the Task above. Then check for errors.

Common errors
Do not use *prefer* after *would rather*.
I **would rather be** *cared for by a robot.* (NOT *I would rather prefer to be . . .*)
Avoid using *rather* before *than* in basic comparisons.
Robots are more suited to heavy work **than** *humans.* (NOT *. . . work rather than . . .*)

Unit 9: Engineering wonders

Vocabulary notebook *How do you do it?*

Learning tip   **Ask a question**

When you learn new vocabulary, put it into a question to ask yourself. Thinking of the question and answer can help you remember it.

Q What's made of steel in the kitchen?
A The silverware / knives and forks.

A   Answer the questions. Use the words in bold in your answers.

1. Is there any **concrete** in the building where you live? _____
2. Are you good at **maneuvering** a car into a small space? _____
3. Are you usually able to **complete** your assignments **on time**? _____
4. Is there an **elevated** highway near your home? _____
5. Have you ever tried to **assemble** flat packed furniture? _____

B   Write questions and answers for these words.

1. construct _____
2. erect _____
3. engineer _____
4. install _____
5. position _____
6. fall behind schedule _____
7. delay _____
8. in a short time frame _____
9. ahead of schedule _____

C   **Word builder** Find the meanings of these words from the article on page 96. Write questions and answers for them.

| to blend into | to float | a landmark | a landscape | a lane | a penalty | a pylon | a viaduct |

A How can new buildings blend into the natural environment?
B Well, using materials in the same colors as those naturally found in an area can help.

D   **Focus on vocabulary** Read the questions below. Replace the verbs in bold with words from the box. Then write your own answers to the questions. Refer to Exercise 2A on page 101 to help you.

| conduct   deployed   determine   identify   interacting   monitor   perform   relate to   transform |

1. What's the best way to **decide** which courses you should take in college?
2. What single thing would **change** your life **completely**?
3. How do you **get along with** people generally? Are you good at **communicating** with others?
4. What jobs in your home would you let a robot **do**?
5. Are you able to **recognize** your own strengths and weaknesses?
6. Have you ever had to **do** a survey for a school project?
7. Which industries are robots best **used** in?
8. How does your boss or professor **watch and check on** your performance?

Checkpoint 3 Units 7–9

1 Is life easier now?

A Rewrite the underlined parts of the sentences, starting with the words in bold. Then complete the missing parts of the expressions.

In this _____ age, many young people may think that life is hard. They **not only** find it difficult to get work, but that it takes time _____ even to get an interview. Young people have **never before** found it so difficult to buy their first home. But maybe we need to _____ think for a moment, because it's **only** by looking back in history that we are able to gain a different perspective.

In the 1930s, people were accustomed to the _____ downs of the stock market, but when it crashed on October 29, 1929, it initiated the Great Depression. The U.S. had **never before** experienced such a catastrophic economic loss, which was coupled with a drought and failure of crops. The Depression **not only** affected the economy, but it also had a huge social impact. People had **rarely** had so little money. It was a time of great pain _____.

Unemployment rates rose above and _____ anything seen previously. Many young men **not only** had to wait to find work before marrying, but many, sick _____ of not being able to find work, migrated in the thousands to other states. Divorce rates had **rarely** been as low as in the 1930s. However, _____ wives often ran away from their marriages. Homelessness became a huge problem. Some people were able to find a roof over their heads **only** by moving in with their relatives.

History shows us that _____ later things can change, and for the 1930s generation, they did – slowly _____. We'll have to _____ see what the next decades will bring us. But one thing is for sure: we move back _____ between good times and hard times.

B **Pair work** Do you think life is difficult for young people? In what ways is life today easier than a hundred years ago? Summarize your points with expressions like *At the end of the day*.

"... When all is said and done, life is a lot easier today than a hundred years ago."

2 Learning lessons from history

Cross out one word to correct the underlined phrases. Rewrite sentences beginning with a bold phrase as a cleft. Rewrite the *italic* sentences without using *if*.

View: How do we approach problems in the world needs to change. We should analyze precisely what are the problems are. Then we should consider whether have there have been similar problems in history. What we do we fail to do is learn lessons from history.

Comment 1: Sir Winston Churchill said, "Those who fail to learn from history are doomed to repeat it." **When we are faced** with a world crisis, we look back and consider how did it happened. **Only several decades ago,** our country suffered a crisis that threatened our security. Yet most people have no idea why do things like that happen. **When people's lives are directly affected,** they pay attention to what's going on in the world.

Comment 2: *If we had learned anything from the twentieth century, this century might be more peaceful.* We should look back before any crisis looms. *If we don't, we are doomed.* And if you should think our problems are new, think again. If you ask any historian, they'll tell you the same problems occur throughout history. *If I were in a position of influence, I'd make history a required subject every year of school.*

3 Improve your relationships

A Complete the article with *whatever, whenever, whoever, whichever, however,* and *wherever*. Then replace the words in bold with one word with a similar meaning.

Problems with a relationship? _____ you look, you'll find advice. But have you tried these tips?

1. _____ you do, don't ignore a problem – no matter how **unimportant** it may seem. If it's a **small** issue, talk it through right away. _____ is at fault, ask what *you* can do to help solve the problem. You'll notice an **instant** change in attitude from your partner.

2. _____ you have an argument, figure out what it is *really* about. Many times they seem to be about something "**on the surface**," but often there's a deeper problem. So focus on _____ *that* problem might be, and _____ you are having an argument about the same old topic, don't just fire off a **quick** answer. Try a different response. You might see a **quick** change in the direction of the argument and a **clear** difference in the outcome. Bad moods are **common**. If your partner is in a bad mood, just remember it's probably **for a short time**. Remember that while there's a **small** chance it's about you, most likely it's not. So _____ it's **obvious** that he or she needs some space, give it to them.

3. _____ the problem, _____ you solve it, use it as a life lesson. Solving even **tiny** problems can create **deep** and lasting changes in your relationships in the future.

B **Pair work** Discuss the advice in Exercise A. What other advice do you have? Use expressions like *considering* and *in light of (the fact that)* to support your opinions.

A However you look at it, you can't really ignore any problem in a relationship.
B Right. I mean, given the fact that you live with someone day after day, it's important to solve problems.

4 Construction projects

A Complete the paragraph with words and expressions. Use the cues given to help you.

Many modern buildings are made of <u>steel</u> and _____ (materials). Sometimes they are _____ (built) or _____ (put together) in one place and then brought to the construction site to be _____ (moved) into position or _____ (put up). After that, all the services need to be _____ (put in). Construction scheduling is a huge challenge. Even though companies agree to complete projects _____ (quickly), their schedules often _____ (are late). This can be because of a _____ (lateness) in getting materials or because the project is complex. For example, roads that are _____ (lifted up) above cities are particularly complex. However, companies often have to pay penalties if the project is not _____ (finish punctually).

B Use the verbs given with perfect infinitives. Then add the expressions in the box. There may be more than one correct answer. Do you have similar views about your city?

| don't get me started | in that case | let's not go there | then | what I'm saying | whatsoever |

Everything's different now. If you look at old photos, the city _____ (seem / change) completely. The old stores _____ (appear / go – I mean, there are none left _____. The old neighborhoods _____ (be supposed to / be) really beautiful, so _____, why did they demolish all the old wooden houses? It's terrible. But _____. I _____ (would love / meet) the planners and asked, "Why did you destroy the character of the city, _____?" They also took out all the trolley cars, which _____ (be said to / be) more environmentally friendly than cars. We need to think about the environment. But _____. We've just lost so much. That's _____.

Checkpoint 3: Units 7–9

Unit 10 Current events

In Unit 10, you...
- talk about news and how it is reported.
- use continuous infinitives to report ongoing events.
- use the subjunctive to write what should happen.
- use *this* and *these* or *that* and *those* in conversation.

Lesson A *Breaking news*

1 Vocabulary in context

A Look at the four headlines. What do you think they are about?

a. *Region still struggling to recover*
b. *Conflict over the economy*
c. *Bomb squad too late*
d. *New contender to enter race?*

B 🔊 CD 4.02 Read the home page of an online news site. Write the headlines in Exercise A in the news articles. Are there any similar events in the news at the moment?

HOME   U.S.   WORLD   POLITICS   JUSTICE   ENTERTAINMENT   LIVING   TRAVEL   OPINION   MONEY   SPORTS >

1. _____
Efforts to **contain the oil spill** on the south coast appear to be working. But the oil giant responsible for the disaster could be facing more difficulties. Local businesses were rumored yesterday to be **considering legal action**, claiming for loss of income and livelihood. "People are going to be suing people over this," said one fisherman. A spokesperson for the oil company said they are committed to **compensating victims** affected by the spill. [Full story]

2. _____
A blast in the downtown area has caused extensive damage. Investigators are not sure what **caused the explosion** but have not **ruled out the possibility** that it was a terrorist attack. Three people were reported to have been acting suspiciously in the financial district, and police were said to be searching for a red pickup truck that was seen in the area. A **bomb went off** in the same area two years ago. [Full story]

3. _____
Three years after becoming the first female senator from her state, a young politician may be preparing to run for office in the upcoming presidential election. While the senator seems not to be **announcing** her **campaign** just yet, an appearance on a Sunday morning talk show has **fueled speculation**. [Full story]
RELATED The president's press secretary announced that the president will be **undergoing routine surgery** later this week and might not be able to greet a trade delegation of Chinese officials. [Full story]

4. _____
Investors might have been worrying unnecessarily after the **stock market plunged** to an all-time low last month. **Stocks** are now **making** a modest **recovery** as **markets** are said to have been gaining in confidence over the last two weeks. However, there are still concerns over the state of the economy and the huge deficits. Protesters are said to be planning more demonstrations in the capital. The marches seem to have been going peacefully so far. However, police say that they will be **mobilizing riot squads** if **tensions escalate**. [Full story]

Word sort

C Make a chart like this of the collocations in bold in the article. Then take turns telling the news stories in Exercise B to a partner.

verb + noun	noun + verb
contain the oil spill	a bomb goes off

Vocabulary notebook
See page 115.

106 Unit 10: Current events

2 Grammar Reporting events in progress

Figure it out

A How are the ideas below expressed in the article? Underline the sentences in the article, and compare them with the sentences below. Then read the grammar chart.

1. They say protesters are planning more demonstrations in the capital.
2. There were rumors yesterday that local businesses are considering legal action.
3. It seems the marches have been going peacefully.
4. It's possible investors have been worrying unnecessarily.

Continuous infinitive forms

Grammar extra See page 162.

Continuous infinitives describe events as ongoing, temporary, or possibly incomplete.
Efforts to contain the oil spill appear **to be working**.
The senator seems **not to be announcing** her campaign just yet.
Police were said **to be searching** for a red pickup truck.
Markets are said **to have been gaining** confidence.

Modals can be followed by *be* + *-ing* or *have been* + *-ing*.
The president **will be undergoing** routine surgery.
Investors **might have been worrying** unnecessarily.

Writing vs. Conversation

In writing, continuous infinitive forms with *to* often come after the verbs *seem, appear, be supposed to, have to*. They are less common in academic writing. In conversation, they are also often used after *be going to, need, want, (have) got to*.

B Complete the news reports using continuous infinitives of the verbs given with or without *to*. Sometimes there is more than one correct answer.

1. The president of an international microchip corporation may _____ (prepare) to step down. Over the last year, his health appears _____ (deteriorate), and the company is now rumored _____ (search) for a successor. A company spokesperson said, "We are going to _____ (make) an announcement soon."
2. After a month of protests, which seem _____ (have) little effect, steel workers agreed yesterday to go back to work. The workers might _____ (try) to get a bigger pay increase, but the company refused to negotiate and appeared _____ (not listen) to their demands.
3. An actor from a popular sitcom might _____ (not appear) on the show again. TV executives are believed _____ (consider) legal action after the actor failed to show up for filming on several occasions. When told the show may _____ (cancel) his contract, the actor said, "You've got to _____ (joke)!"
4. A senator who was filmed last week at a nightclub when she should _____ (attend) government meetings would make no comment today. An opposition spokesperson said that she was supposed to _____ (represent) voters in her state that evening.

HMM. IT SAYS HERE THAT NEW COFFEE YOU'RE DRINKING MAY BE KEEPING YOU UP AT NIGHT.

3 Viewpoint

Pair work Choose a story that's in the news at the moment. Prepare a news report to present to the class. Give as much detail as you can.

"Fans of the biggest sitcom on television may have been protesting unnecessarily. The show's producers announced that they are going to be bring the show back for at least one more season."

Lesson B "Old" news

1 Grammar in context

A Where do you get your news from? Conventional, mainstream sources or via social networking? Do a class survey.

"I tend to read the headlines on my phone every morning."

B 🔊 CD 4.03 Read the editorial column. What is "old" news? How does the writer regard it?

Why it is essential that "old" news survive

In the United States, in the trial of a celebrity on a murder charge, a judge demands that the jury reach its verdict. On the other side of the world, a devastating earthquake strikes. In Europe, the winning goal is scored in a crucial soccer game. All three events are instantly broadcast around the world – not via conventional news media, but through text messages, microblogs, social network postings, emails, and blogs that are passed on, person to person, within seconds. The major news organizations receive the same news from their reporters, but because of their insistence that everything be written and edited to broadcast standards, by the time it is broadcast or posted on the Web, it has become "old" news, if only by a few minutes.

In a world where readers and viewers get news via their smartphones and social media, it is important that the story be instantly available. Meanwhile, the requirement that a journalist check the facts more conscientiously can mean precious time is lost. In the case of major breaking news, the mainstream news organizations may insist that a controversial story be investigated, even if this means a delay in broadcasting some of the details. In dangerous situations, it may be advisable that a foreign correspondent not go to the scene immediately. It is essential that the reputation of the organization not be damaged and that the safety of the reporter be guaranteed.

In light of this situation, there is a danger that the major news organizations are perceived as a source of old news, which only a few might turn to for the fuller details of events they already know about. However, it is essential that there be a place for news that, while slower, is ultimately more measured, in-depth, and trustworthy. Ultimately, this comes down to money and whether the public is prepared to pay for such meticulously researched content. It is crucial that this issue be taken seriously by all consumers of news before we lose something precious.

C **Pair work** Discuss the questions.

1. Why are conventional news sources sometimes slower?
2. What qualities does "old" news have?
3. Do you recognize the picture the editorial paints of news? Do you think it's accurate?
4. What do you think is the real purpose of the editorial? What does it want you, the reader, to do?
5. What do you think about the recommendation?

2 Grammar Describing what should happen

Figure it out

A Write the form of the verb given that the editorial writer uses to express these ideas. Then read the grammar chart.

1. The judge demands that the jury _____ its verdict. (reach)
2. The requirement that a journalist _____ the facts can mean time is lost. (check)
3. It is important that the story _____ instantly available. (be)

The subjunctive

Grammar extra See page 163.

The subjunctive uses the base form of the verb. Use it for all persons – including third person singular – after certain verbs, nouns, and adjectives. You can use it to refer to demands, suggestions, and recommendations; to say what is important; or to say what should happen in an ideal world

Verbs: demand, insist, require, request, ask, suggest, recommend

The judge demands that the jury **reach** its verdict.
They insist that everything **be edited**.

Nouns: demand, requirement, insistence, suggestion, recommendation

The requirement that a journalist **check** the facts can mean time is lost.

Adjectives: important, crucial, necessary, advisable, essential

It is important that the story **be** instantly available.

The negative form is *not* + verb.

It is essential that its reputation **not be damaged**.

Writing vs. Conversation

The subjunctive is rare in conversation. People say:
*The judge asked the jury **to reach** its verdict.*
*It's important that the story **should be / is** accurate.*

B Read the comments below. Then complete the editorial extracts that reflect these views. Use the subjunctive form of the underlined verbs in the comments.

1. Parents say: "Our kids aren't <u>aware</u> of world events." "They're not <u>exposed</u> to 'proper news' early enough." "We want schools to <u>teach</u> current events." "They should <u>make</u> it a priority."

Parents are demanding that their children _____ well-informed about world events. Many feel it is important that children from sixth grade on _____ to reputable news sources. Their insistence that the school curriculum _____ students current events is right. It is our recommendation that every school _____ this a priority.

2. Students say: "Local news needs to <u>change</u>." "They should <u>include</u> more news about us." "The local TV station should <u>have</u> reports on our activities." "Don't <u>ignore</u> us."

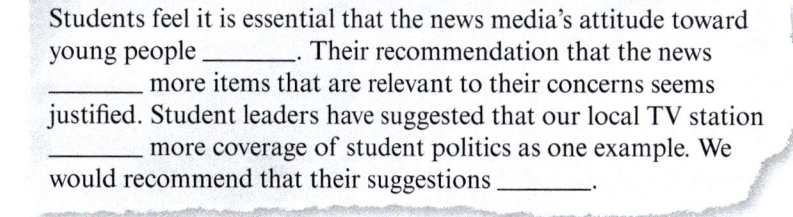

Students feel it is essential that the news media's attitude toward young people _____. Their recommendation that the news _____ more items that are relevant to their concerns seems justified. Student leaders have suggested that our local TV station _____ more coverage of student politics as one example. We would recommend that their suggestions _____.

3. Media experts say: "Newspapers shouldn't <u>die</u>." "They should <u>change</u> their business model." "The consumer should <u>pay</u> more for access to online news."

It is crucial to the well-being of society that newspapers _____, but they do need to change. The suggestion that the traditional business model _____ should be taken seriously. It is time to insist that the consumer _____ more for access to high-quality news reports.

About you

C Write an editorial about an issue that you feel strongly about. Share it with the class.

Lesson C Those news tickers

1 Conversation strategy Highlighting topics

A How often do you listen to or watch the news? Are you a "news junkie"?

B 🔊 CD 4.04 Listen. How do Jill and Kyung get their news?

Jill	Have you noticed how some people seem almost addicted to news? Like, this guy at work, he has all these news apps on his phone, but he never knows what's going on, really.
Kyung	Yeah. My girlfriend, she watches news channels all the time. But I don't think she really listens, you know what I mean? It's just background noise.
Jill	I know. Those TV channels, they just repeat the same news over and over. It drives me crazy, hearing the same thing all the time.
Kyung	Me too. And those news tickers, they're another thing I hate. It's so distracting, trying to listen with those things going across the screen at the same time.
Jill	Yeah. Public radio, that's what I like. They have some really interesting in-depth reports, too.
Kyung	Speaking of which, did you hear that report about that huge investment company? It seems to be going under.

C **Notice** how Jill and Kyung highlight the topics they talk about. Sometimes they put the topic at the start of a sentence and then use a pronoun. Sometimes they put the topic at the end. Find more examples in the conversation.

> **My girlfriend, she** watches news channels all the time.
> **It** drives me crazy, **hearing the same thing all the time.**

> **In conversation . . .**
> When speakers put a topic at the end, it's usually after an evaluative comment such as *It drives me crazy*.
> **Note:** These structures are for use in conversation only. Do not use them in writing.

D 🔊 CD 4.05 Guess the missing topics in these sentences. Then listen and write the topics.

1. _____, that's another thing people listen to but can never remember afterwards.
2. _____ these days, it always seems to be reporting what's going to happen. It's annoying.
3. _____, that's beyond me. I don't understand anything about the markets and trade.
4. _____, it's more informative than TV news. The reports are just more in-depth.
5. _____, they're all I read these days. I never have time to read the full articles or news stories.
6. It's fantastic, having _____ on your phone. You can keep up with the news wherever you are.
7. It takes up so much airtime, _____. Especially if you're not interested in football or whatever.
8. They're so dirty and difficult to handle, _____. I don't miss them at all.

About you **E** **Pair work** Discuss the statements in Exercise D. Do you agree?

Unit 10: Current events

2 Strategy plus *this, that, these, those*

CD 4.06 You can use *this* and *these* to introduce and highlight important information.

This guy at work, he has all **these** news apps.

Did you hear **that** report?

You can use *that* and *those* to refer to something specific, which you have mentioned or expect your listener to know about.

You can use *that* and *those* to sound negative about a topic.

Those news tickers, they're another thing I hate.

A **CD 4.07** Complete these comments with *this, that, these,* or *those.* Use the cues in parentheses. Then listen and check.

1. There's _____ show on the radio called *Radio Lab*. It has _____ really interesting, creative reports on things like time, or ants, or numbers. It's so cool. Do you listen to the radio much? (*highlight*)
2. There were all _____ students in my high school who had no idea what was going on in the world. (*highlight*) To them, international news was boring. Do you follow international news?
3. You know _____ talk show host on late night TV? I don't like her interview style. (*sound negative*) I don't think talk show hosts should be aggressive. What do you think?
4. I hate _____ magazines that make up news like celebrity gossip or stuff that you *know* isn't true. (*be specific*) Don't you?

About you

B **Pair work** Ask and answer the questions at the end of each comment above.

3 Strategies and listening *Journalism*

A Look at some of the issues in journalism. What do you think they refer to?

"The first issue is probably about the fact that news is often reported instantaneously."

1. ☐ The speed at which news is reported
2. ☐ The cost of publishing news stories
3. ☐ The increase in the number of news sources
4. ☐ 24-hour rolling news reports are superficial.
5. ☐ The use of graphic photos
6. ☐ The influence of reporters on events

B **CD 4.08** Listen to a radio show. Which trends do the speakers refer to? Check (✓) the topics in Exercise A.

C **CD 4.09** Listen again. Circle the correct option to complete each sentence. Then discuss the expert's views with a partner. Do you agree?

1. The radio presenter suggests that journalists' work is often _____.
   a. mundane   b. risky   c. boring   d. fun
2. The expert says that journalists often publish their reports _____.
   a. as events take place   b. through agencies   c. 24 hours later   d. before something happens
3. The expert suggests that the reason news organizations use some pictures is _____.
   a. they want to shock   b. it's ethically right   c. to show the truth   d. to compete
4. The expert believes that journalists can _____.
   a. change situations   b. have a huge impact   c. have limited influence   d. give no personal views

Speaking naturally
See page 142.

Unit 10: Current events   111

Lesson D Reporting the news

1 Reading

A Prepare Are some sources of news more trustworthy than others? In what ways?

"I think the news on public radio is pretty reliable because..."

B **Read for main ideas** Read the article. What kinds of information does the writer question in terms of its accuracy? Why is information sometimes not accurate?

Establishing the truth: How accurate are news reports?

1 Following one of the worst natural disasters in recent U.S. history – Hurricane Katrina – journalists and newscasters swarmed the area to report on the extraordinarily terrible events. There were stories of chaos: widespread looting, gunshots, murders, and other violent crimes. While there was indeed disorder, it turned out that much of the initial reporting was either exaggerated, misleading, or plain wrong. The murder victims didn't materialize, and it became apparent there was no widespread increase in violent crime, either.

2 This episode raises some important questions. How does such "news" get reported? Can we believe what we hear on breaking news, or is news reporting so overstated that we are being at best misinformed and at worst deceived? How do we ultimately know whether any of the so-called facts in a news report are true or misrepresented? And perhaps more importantly, how can we verify what we read or hear in news reports?

3 In the case of Hurricane Katrina, a complex mix of circumstances may have created a degree of misinformation. Immediately after the storm, power outages and breakdowns in communications systems caused news "blackouts," making reliable information extremely difficult, if not almost impossible, to establish. News was spread by word of mouth, and it seems that facts became distorted as they were passed along. However, some of the blame may also lie with how news organizations operate. On the air 24/7, they are under pressure to fill airtime and win viewer ratings by being the one with the "hottest" or latest story. It is easy to see how, under such pressure, events are reported without the facts being painstakingly checked.

4 Such distortions are not limited to headline news events. During an election year, one takes for granted that candidates try to boost their ratings in the opinion polls in an effort to swing the race. The public is used to hearing claims from candidates, such as how their policies have led to an increase in manufacturing jobs or how the opposition has created massive national debt. What the public is never quite certain of is what is truth, half-truth, or untruth. Not surprising, then, that an entire industry exists to answer these very questions. Enter the fact-checkers, who check the claims that are made and the accuracy of the statistics that are presented.

5 Indeed, websites have sprung up whose business is purely and simply to check information in the public sphere – whether it be in a news report, a magazine article, or an urban myth. Other consumer sites aim to reduce the level of deception in politics, and some claim to be able to show the extent to which you can believe certain speechmakers. Cable networks also realize that the public is increasingly concerned about being able to trust what they hear, and use slogans to impress on their viewers the fact that they present honest news that is balanced and without bias. While many have jumped on the bandwagon of truth, one enterprising website has done the complete opposite. Rather than publish verifiable facts, it prides itself on featuring satirical news stories which are completely fabricated. Unfortunately, not all media outlets have realized this, and on occasion they have cited reports from the website as though they were true. Sorting fact from fiction just became even more of a challenge.

> **Reading tip**
> Writers sometimes start an article with a short story to illustrate what they are going to write about.

C Understanding idioms What does the writer mean by saying . . .

1. breakdowns in communications systems caused news "blackouts"? (para. 3)
2. news was passed by "word of mouth"? (para. 3)
3. in an effort to "swing the race"? (para. 4)
4. websites have "sprung up"? (para. 5)
5. many have "jumped on the bandwagon" of truth? (para. 5)

D Read for inference Check (✓) the statements that the writer would agree with.

1. ☐ Hurricane Katrina caused an increase in crime.
2. ☐ There are several reasons why the facts are sometimes misrepresented.
3. ☐ It is difficult to tell truth from fiction in modern news reporting.
4. ☐ It is only major events that are not reported truthfully.
5. ☐ The general public needs consumer websites to know if politicians are telling the truth.
6. ☐ These websites really make politicians more truthful.
7. ☐ It is much easier these days to determine if information is accurate.
8. ☐ The news on one satirical news website is more truthful than from other media outlets.

2 Focus on vocabulary Truth or fiction?

> **Tip**
> Prefixes sometimes help you understand meanings: *mis-* often means "badly."

A Find alternative ways in the article to express the ideas below. Compare with a partner.

Talking about truth . . .
make sure something is true (para. 2)
find out (facts) (para. 3)
truth or correctness (para. 4)
believe in (para. 5)

. . . and lies
giving a wrong impression (para. 1)
exaggerated (para. 2)
lied to (para. 2)
presented in a false way (para. 2)
wrong information (para. 3)
changed to be untrue (para. 3)
an untrue story (para. 5)
made up (para. 5)

B Make a chart like the one below of the words you found in Exercise A. Add other forms. Write (–) if you cannot make the word into a noun, an adjective, or a verb.

Noun	Adjective	Verb
verification		

About you

C Pair work Discuss the questions. Try to use at least six of the new words.

- Does the situation the article describes apply to news organizations you follow?
- Do you always trust everything you hear or read?
- Have you ever found something in the news to be exaggerated or misleading?
- Do you think news stories about celebrities are fabricated? What else is?
- Which news channels do people trust most?
- Do you enjoy satirical news websites or TV shows? If so, which ones?

Writing *In short, . . .*

In this lesson, you . . .
- summarize an article.
- choose singular or plural verbs.
- avoid errors with verbs in relative clauses.

Task Write a summary.

Write a summary of the article on page 112 in no more than 150 words.

A Look at a model Read the summary below of the article on page 112 and the notes. Cross out two sentences in the summary that are not suitable. Then circle the correct verbs.

Writing a summary
Use your own words.
Include main points only.
Do not add new ideas.
Do not add an opinion.

It is crucial that news reporting be accurate. The dramatic news reports after Hurricane Katrina, some of which **was / were** later shown to be inaccurate, **is / are** an example of the difficulties of news reporting. The reasons for inaccurate news coverage **varies / vary**. In complex situations, news **is / are** easily misreported, owing to a variety of factors.

Social networks seem to be taking over news reporting. People often **pass / passes** on inaccuracies in word-of-mouth reporting, while in places of conflict, there can be failures in power and communications. News organizations **bear / bears** some responsibility for inaccurate reporting because they do not always verify facts. Political reporting and campaigning **is / are** also in danger of misleading the public and **has / have** led to the need for professional fact-checkers. The number of websites which **checks / check** facts in the news **has / have** grown as a result of increasing public concern.

B Focus on language Read the chart. Then complete the sentences below with simple present verbs.

Subject-verb agreement in writing

Use singular verbs after uncountable nouns and most singular nouns that refer to a group.
News is easily misreported. **Information needs** to be checked. **The public is** concerned.

Use a singular verb if the main noun in a phrase is singular, but not in expressions that mean "a lot of."
The **number** of websites . . . **has** grown.   BUT   A number of websites **have** appeared.

Use a plural verb after noun *and* noun, when the main noun is plural, and after an irregular plural noun.
Political **reporting and campaigning are** in danger of misleading the public.
The **reasons** for inaccurate news coverage **are** varied. **People pass** on inaccuracies.

1. People _____ to be able to trust the organizations that _____ news. (need / broadcast)
2. The main reason for inaccuracies _____ that news reports and broadcasts _____ live. (be)
3. The number of reporters who _____ accurate accounts of stories _____ every year. (give / grow)
4. Accurate news and information _____ hard to find. The pressure on reporters _____ huge. (be)
5. A number of journalists _____ always _____ news accurately. (not report)
6. The population generally _____ to know the truth, even if the truth _____ not easy to hear. (want / be)
7. The use of social networks _____ news reporting. (affect)

C Write and check Write a summary of the article on page 112. Then check for errors.

Common errors
Be careful with the verbs in relative clauses.
*The number of websites which **check** news **has** grown. (NOT . . . ~~checks~~ . . . ~~have~~)*

Unit 10: Current events

Vocabulary notebook *Trust your instincts.*

Learning tip **Verb + noun collocations**

When you learn a new verb + noun expression, find other verbs that collocate with the noun.

perform / undergo / have / routine surgery

Dictionary tip

Read all the examples in a dictionary entry for a word. They often give clues to collocations.

surgery /ˈsɜr·dʒə·ri/ *n* [C/U]

the treatment of injuries or diseases by cutting open the body and removing or repairing the damaged part, or an operation of this type:

[U] *He had undergone open-heart surgery two years ago.*

[U] *I'm recovering from back surgery, so it's going to be awhile before I can ride a horse again.*

[C] *She has undergone several surgeries and will require more.*

A Which two verbs go with each noun in bold below? Circle a, b, or c.

1. a. contain   b. hold   c. prevent   **an oil spill**
2. a. rule   b. contemplate c. consider   **legal action**
3. a. compensate   b. create   c. protect   **victims**
4. a. mobilize   b. trigger   c. cause   **an explosion**
5. a. explore   b. edit   c. rule out   **the possibility**
6. a. run   b. announce   c. determine   **a campaign**
7. a. fuel   b. make   c. cause   **speculation**
8. a. do   b. make   c. see   **a recovery**

B Find two verbs in the box that can be used to complete each sentence below.

| arise | called in | escalate | explode | go | go off | mobilized | plummet | plunge | start |

1. Bombs can _____ or _____.
2. The stock market can _____ or _____.
3. Protest marches can _____ or _____ peacefully.
4. Riot squads can be _____ or _____.
5. Tensions can _____ or _____.

C **Focus on vocabulary** Complete the vocabulary notes with words from Lesson D on page 113. Look for words with similar meanings to the words in bold.

1. **confirm** or **prove** or _____ the accuracy of a story, someone's identity
2. **find out** or _____ the facts, the truth, someone's identity
3. **believe (in)** or _____ your instincts, your judgment
4. **exaggerate** or _____ the impact or benefits of something
5. **lie to** or _____ the public, consumers, voters
6. **not tell the truth about** or _____ information, facts, someone's position or view
7. paint an **unclear** or _____ picture or give a **false** or _____ impression
8. create or perpetuate an **untrue story** or an urban _____
9. **make up** or _____ evidence, stories, an account, a report

11 Is it real?

In Unit 11, you . . .
- talk about whether information is true or not.
- use *be to* expressions to talk about the future.
- use passive verb complements.
- express concerns with expressions like *That's my concern.*
- give your opinion using *To me.*

Lesson A *Imagined threats?*

1 Grammar in context

A What kinds of threats to society are there? What could disrupt life as we know it? Make a list.

B 🔊 CD 4.10 Read the blog. What threats does it mention? Are any of the threats on your list?

WHAT ARE WE TO BELIEVE?

Recently I saw a trailer for a TV documentary that is to air later this week. It's about families known as "preppers." These are people who are so convinced that life as we know it is to end or that civilization is about to collapse that they are preparing for the day it happens. So they're stockpiling food, water, and survival equipment, which no one is to touch until the day when some unknown disaster occurs – like the failure of the national grid, a natural disaster, even an asteroid strike – which they say is bound to happen eventually. I have to admit: If society were to collapse tomorrow, or if food and energy supplies were to be threatened, they are certainly better prepared than my family. We have barely three cans of baked beans and a pack of birthday candles between us. If we are to survive a catastrophe, we'd better shape up.

If the doomsayers are correct, the world as we know it is to end sooner than we think – which kind of got me thinking about what threats to our lives are real and which are imagined.

For example, remember Y2K? At the turn of this century, there was a great panic that computer systems around the world were about to crash because of the way computers recognized dates. The Year 2000, or Y2K, as it became commonly known, was set to be the biggest systems failure the world had ever experienced. It never happened.

Another perceived threat is an asteroid strike. Is one imminent? If so, shouldn't we all be panicking? Didn't the last one wipe out the dinosaurs? Well, according to experts at NASA*, earth is not about to be hit by an asteroid. They do say that there's bound to be debris from space falling on us at some point, although given the fact that around 70 percent of the earth's surface is water, there's little chance it's going to fall on me as I head for the supermarket.

There's always some disaster that's about to happen. And it truly is hard to know what's real and what's not. So what's the average family like us to do? Maybe the next time I go to the supermarket, I'll buy a few more cans of baked beans and some large white regular candles. Just in case.

*National Aeronautics and Space Administration

END OF WORLD AHEAD

C **Pair work** Discuss the questions.

1. What kind of blog is this? Instructive? Lighthearted? Informative?
2. What kinds of things are "preppers" stockpiling? What other things might they need?
3. Why does the writer suggest we ought to be panicking? Do situations like that cause you to panic?
4. Have you prepared in any way for problems that may arise in the future? How?

2 Grammar Talking about the future

Figure it out

A Find the underlined ideas in the blog and rewrite the sentences. Then read the chart.

1. Life as we know it will end.
2. Civilization is going to collapse very soon.
3. It's certain there will be debris from space.

Expressions with *be to*

Grammar extra See page 164.

You can use *be to* to refer to the immediate future, especially events that are fixed or decided.
A TV documentary **is to air** later this week.

You can also use *be to* in conditional sentences and for hypothetical events in the future.
If we **are to survive** a catastrophe, we'd better shape up.
If society **were to collapse**, these people are well prepared.

Be about to means something will happen very soon; *be bound to* or *be set to* suggest certainty.
Civilization **is not about to collapse**. There**'s bound to be** debris falling on us.

These expressions can also be used to talk about the future as it was seen in the past.
They said the world **was to end** in 2012. It **was bound to happen**, they said.

B Complete the sentences from a survey using the words given. Then ask and answer the questions. Do situations like these concern you?

If scientists are right, a global flu pandemic _____ (bound) occur sooner or later. Some years ago, a flu virus that _____ (set) affect millions of people turned out to be less disastrous than predicted. If another pandemic _____ (be) occur, would you panic?
A super volcano in North America _____ (set) explode sometime in the future. It's not known when, but an eruption is 40,000 years overdue if past patterns _____ (be) be repeated. If you _____ (about) travel to that area soon, would you cancel your trip?
Doomsayers predict that cyber-warfare _____ (bound) happen soon. They're not the only ones who think that computer systems _____ (set) fail as a result of infiltration. Security experts say that if cyber-terrorists _____ (be) attack, we would not be prepared.

3 Viewpoint Are you prepared?

Group work Discuss the questions below.

In conversation . . .
You can introduce what you say with an adverb (e.g., *clearly, fortunately*) to show your attitude.

- Have you ever had to evacuate a building for any reason? Do you know what you're supposed to do in a fire drill?
- If communications systems were to shut down around the country, what would you do? How would it affect you?
- Do you know what people are to do if utility supplies shut off for any reason? What problems would the loss of utilities be bound to cause?
- If you were to hear of an impending crisis (such as a hurricane), how would you prepare?
- What supplies should people have ready in these situations?

"Interestingly enough, we had to evacuate our office building one time. Luckily, it was OK in the end."

Unit 11: Is it real? 117

Lesson B Hard to believe

1 Vocabulary in context

A 🔊 CD 4.11 Read the article. What is Frank Abagnale known for — now and in the past?

Why Frank W. Abagnale deserves to be admired

Frank Abagnale is a well-respected businessman, but **turn back the clock** several decades and you will find a notorious past – a past that he probably never expected to be **turned into** a Hollywood movie. But it's his work over the last four decades with the FBI* and other agencies – after he **turned his back on** a life of crime – that he'd rather be remembered for.

As one of the world's most respected authorities on security and fraud prevention, Abagnale is the person to **turn to** when you need to understand the crimes of check forgery and embezzlement. That's because he was an expert at these activities. In his youth, Abagnale was an extraordinary con artist, successfully conning people into thinking he was an airline pilot, a pediatrician, and a college professor – without ever being qualified in any of these fields. He lived a jet-setting lifestyle, but it **turned out** that he had funded all his activities by forging checks across the globe. He successfully avoided being apprehended for several years but was finally caught at the age of 21 by French authorities. He served prison time in three different countries. It was a **turning point** in his life.

Abagnale recalls being devastated by his parents' divorce, shortly after which he started his life of deception. His crimes, committed between the ages of 16 and 21, earned him a 12-year U.S. prison term, which seems to have been considered harsh even back then. He ended up being released early after agreeing to assist U.S. federal law enforcement agencies. It was an offer Abagnale was smart enough not to **turn down**, and it allowed him to **turn over a new leaf** in his life.

Even if you can't **turn a blind eye** to his past, Abagnale deserves to be admired for the way he **turned** his life **around**. On his website, he states that he regrets being drawn into illegal and unethical activities. He comments, too, on the movie *Catch Me If You Can*, which is loosely based on his life. Abagnale wants it to be known that it's not a true biography. Indeed, many of the events appear to have been exaggerated, which can only be expected. After all, it is a movie.

―――――――――――――――――――――――
*the Federal Bureau of Investigation – a U.S. government agency

Word sort

B Find idioms and phrasal verbs with *turn* in the article that have the meanings below.

1. stop being involved in _____
2. become _____
3. stop a bad habit _____
4. ignore _____
5. a moment of change _____
6. refuse _____
7. go back in time _____
8. become apparent _____
9. make something better _____
10. go to, approach _____

C **Pair work** Discuss the questions. How many *turn* expressions can you use?

1. Why does Frank Abagnale have a "notorious" past? Why is he now a respected authority on security?
2. When did he begin his life of deception? How did he turn his life around?
3. What do you think about the way Abagnale turned over a new leaf?
4. Have you seen *Catch Me If You Can*? If not, would you like to?

Vocabulary notebook
See page 125.

Unit 11: Is it real?

2 Grammar Information focus

Figure it out

A Which of the two options in each sentence is the idea that is expressed in the article? What's the difference in meaning between the two options? Then read the grammar chart.

1. It's his work for the FBI that Abagnale would rather **remember / be remembered for**.
2. He has a notorious past, which he never expected **to be turned / to turn** into a movie.
3. Many of the events appear **to be exaggerated / to have been exaggerated**.
4. He regrets **drawing others / being drawn** into illegal activities.

Passive verb complements

Grammar extra See page 165.

Base forms, infinitives, and *-ing* forms can have passive forms after some verbs and expressions.

Base form	He'd rather **be remembered** for his work with the FBI. (= i.e., that others remember him.)
	He'd rather **remember** his work with the FBI. (= He prefers to remember it himself.)
Infinitives	Abagnale deserves **to be admired**. (= Other people should admire him.)
	A 12-year prison term appears **to have been considered** harsh even then.
-ing form	He avoided **being apprehended** for several years.

Use base forms after *had better*, *would rather*, and modal verbs.
Use infinitives after *appear*, *claim*, *deserve*, *expect*, *love*, etc., *seem*, *want*, *'d like*.
Use *-ing* forms after *avoid*, *be worth*, *enjoy*, *love*, etc., *mind*, *recall*, *remember*, *regret*.

B Complete what these people say about a movie of their lives. Use passive verb complements of the verbs given. Sometimes there is more than one correct answer.

If they made a movie of my life, . . .

1. I'd rather _____ (play) by Chris Rock than anyone else. I want _____ (remember) for my humor, and he's a funny guy. I wouldn't mind _____ (play) by Eddie Murphy, either.
2. One thing I'd really like _____ (know) for is being kind to people. I'd rather _____ (remember) for that than for the hours I spend at work.
3. I took my math exams three times to improve my grade. That deserves _____ (include) in a movie about me!
4. Don't show my first job – I never expected _____ (fire). I hate _____ (tell) what to do and I argued with my boss. I was right, but it wasn't worth _____ (fire) for.
5. One story about me that should never _____ (tell) is the time I stole money from my mother's purse. Fortunately, it seems _____ (forget). I'm sure she'd rather not _____ (remind) of it in the movie.
6. I've always avoided _____ (make) to do things that I don't want to do. That's one thing I'd like _____ (say) about me.
7. I'd like _____ (give) the chance to direct the movie. I might _____ (nominate) for "best director." I'd enjoy _____ (present) with an award!

About you

C Imagine a movie being made of your life. Make the sentences above true for you. Then share your ideas with a partner.

"I think one thing I'd really like to be known for is being a good friend."

Speaking naturally
See page 143.

Unit 11: Is it real? 119

Lesson C *That's my concern.*

1 Conversation strategy Expressing concerns

A A "white lie" is often told to be tactful or polite. In what kinds of situations might someone tell a "white lie"? Would you ever call someone on telling a white lie? (= point it out)

"For example, if an older person asked me to guess their age, I might say they're younger."

B 🔊 CD 4.12 Listen. What does Tania think about telling lies? How about Tom?

Tania You know, it's interesting. A friend of mine was telling her 12-year-old son about how it's not good to tell lies, and then he caught her telling a lie.

Tom He did not.

Tania Oh, yeah. They were going into an amusement park, and she told them he was 11 to get the reduced rate. And her son called her on it.

Tom Well, yeah. I mean, that doesn't seem right.

Tania Yeah. And she's like, "It's just a white lie." I guess, to her, it was no big deal. But you know, I'm not comfortable with that. To me, it was a lie.

Tom Yeah, very much so, but . . . did you tell her that?

Tania No. I just laughed it off.

Tom See, that doesn't sit quite right with me.

Tania But what are you supposed to do? Say, "That's wrong"?

Tom Yeah, but I mean, if you don't say anything, that's kind of a lie, too. That would be my concern, anyhow.

C **Notice** how Tania and Tom use expressions like these to express their concerns. Find the examples they use in the conversation.

That's not good.	I'm not too happy about (that).
That's my concern.	I'm not comfortable with (that).
That doesn't seem right.	That doesn't sit right with me.

D 🔊 CD 4.13 Listen. Complete the conversations with the expressions you hear.

1. **A** You know what I don't like? When people realize they've done something wrong, and then they don't tell the whole story – you know, to try and hide it. _____.
   B Yeah. _____. That's kind of like lying, too, when you don't tell the whole story.

2. **A** What do you do if you find out your friend's boyfriend is cheating on her? Do you tell her?
   B No. _____. I mean, it's not your business. It's better not to get involved.
   A Yeah, but _____ – not saying something.

3. **A** So if someone asks you, "Does this look good?" and it looks awful, what would you say? I mean, you can't say it looks terrible. You'd hurt their feelings. _____.
   B Yeah, but you can still say it looks awful but in a tactful way. Like, "Your other one looks way better."

About you **E** **Pair work** Discuss the conversations above. What are your views?

Unit 11: Is it real?

2 Strategy plus *To me, ...*

CD 4.14 You can use **to me** to mean "that's how it seems to me," "that's my view."

To me, it was a lie.

You can also use **to** + other pronouns or nouns.

To her, / To my friend, it was no big deal.

A ◆ CD 4.15 Listen to five people talk about white lies. Number the responses 1–5.

☐ Right. And you don't want to risk your friendship over something so minor. To me, it's not worth it.
☐ Maybe to them, it's a way of trying to make friends, like saying, "Look, I'm worth knowing."
☐ Yeah. To him, that's not a lie. He's just telling a story, and he's getting a bit carried away.
☐ Very much so. In any case, is that really a lie? To me, it's just a case of believing in yourself.
☐ I agree. Saying something's nice is a relatively minor thing to me. Like, it doesn't hurt anyone

About you

B ◆ CD 4.16 **Pair work** Listen again and discuss each response. Do you agree with the speakers?

3 Listening and strategies Online lies

A ◆ CD 4.17 Read the start of a conversation. Can you guess the missing words? Then listen and write the missing information.

A Do you think most people post things on social network sites that are untrue?
B Not sure. I know I have. I've listed a _____, and I actually use a _____. And to me, that's OK. I'm just protecting _____. I mean, some people change things like their marital status. But that doesn't sit right with me – saying you're single when you're actually married.
A So have you ever changed other information, like, you know, your _____ or ... ?

B ◆ CD 4.18 Listen to the rest of the conversation. How do the speakers answer the questions below?

1. Why is it easier to lie online than in person?
2. What's the biggest lie people tell face-to-face?
3. What kinds of white lies do people tell on online dating sites?
4. Are men or women more likely to tell white lies?
5. How can you tell if someone is lying in person? What do they do?

About you

C **Pair work** Discuss the questions in Exercises A and B. What are your views? Give examples of people you know or stories you've heard.

A I know people who have posted stuff on their profiles that's not true. But it seems silly to me.
B Well, the problem is everyone has access to that information and ...

Unit 11: Is it real? 121

Lesson D Artistic fakes

1 Reading

A Prepare Look at the title of the article and the photographs. Brainstorm 10 words that you might read in the article. Make a list.

painting
forgery

B Read for main ideas Read the article. What techniques are used to authenticate art?

Authenticating ART

1 When a work of art sells at auction for millions of dollars, the buyer needs to be certain of its authenticity. Establishing this is not always straightforward, and therefore it is not uncommon for forged works of art to change hands for large sums of money, earning the forger or corrupt dealer huge profits. Forgery can be a lucrative business. Museums, galleries, and private collectors all over the world have repeatedly been taken in by art forgeries despite their best efforts to authenticate the artwork, as this almost unbelievable story illustrates.

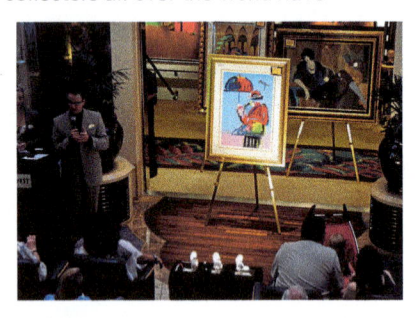

2 Several decades ago, a New York art dealer bought three watercolors, which he believed to have been painted by the famous Russian artist Marc Chagall. The fact that they were fakes may never have come to light had the dealer not met with the artist that very same day, entirely by chance. Chagall reportedly declared the paintings to be fake immediately on seeing them. The man who sold the art, and who also happened to be the forger, served several years in prison as a result of his dishonesty.

3 However, most dealers are not this fortunate, and in most cases experts are unable to rely on the word of the actual artist to determine whether a piece of artwork is authentic. In the past, it was art experts and academics who were the main sources for authentication, rather than scientific proof. Other methods of authenticating art include tracing its ownership, a laborious and often unreliable process, especially if the work is several centuries old.

4 While these methods of verifying a work of art remain important, experts also rely on a variety of other techniques, such as analyzing the handwriting of the artist's signature. More technological approaches include carbon dating the pigments in the paint or the age of a canvas. In one case of a painting whose origin was uncertain but thought to be that of Leonardo da Vinci, a high-resolution multi-spectral camera was used to identify a faint fingerprint on the canvas. The fingerprint was then matched to another on a known work of da Vinci's. Carbon dating of the canvas also matched with material of the same period – around 1500. With such techniques, the painting's authenticity seemed to have been confirmed, although there are still those who fiercely contest it.

5 More recently, experts have turned to digital-imaging techniques to examine works of art in fine detail, such as the brushstroke patterns in a painting. In one study, analysts scanned 23 genuine van Gogh works into a computer and studied the number of brushstrokes they had, their length and how steadily they had been made. Statistical models were then developed to create a unique "signature" of the work. Works of art that were known to have been forged were found to have more brushstrokes when compared to genuine works.

6 The difference in value between a forgery and a genuine piece can run into millions of dollars, so there's a lot at stake. Not only that, but anyone who appreciates art wants to see the handiwork of the original artist and not be fooled by the copycat efforts of a forger. However, experts now have a growing arsenal of forensic techniques, which may well make it harder to pass off forged works of art in the future.

Reading tip
Writers often use the first paragraph of a text to set out a problem to which the rest of the text will offer solutions.

C **Read for detail** Answer the questions about the article.

1. What is not uncommon in the art world?
2. How was the Chagall forgery uncovered?
3. Why has authenticating art been unreliable in the past?
4. How can experts tell if a van Gogh painting is genuine?
5. Why is it important to be certain about a work of art's authenticity?

D **Read for inference** Are the sentences below true (T) or false (F) or is the information not given (NG)? Write T, F, or NG.

1. It's easy to make money from forging art. _____
2. The New York art dealer was a longtime friend of Marc Chagall. _____
3. The New York art dealer had arranged to meet Marc Chagall after he bought the paintings. _____
4. Few experts are as lucky as the New York art dealer. _____
5. Experts all agree that the da Vinci painting is authentic. _____
6. Van Gogh's signature was analyzed on 23 of his paintings. _____

2 Focus on vocabulary Words in context

A What do the words in bold mean? Which parts of the article help you guess their meaning? Explain your guesses to a partner.

> **Tip**
> If you don't understand a word, look back or ahead in the text for clues to help you.

1. Forgery can be a **lucrative** business. (para. 1)
2. Collectors all over the world have repeatedly been **taken in** by art forgeries. (para. 1)
3. The fact that they were fakes may never have **come to light**. (para. 2)
4. . . . **tracing** the ownership of a piece of art can help to determine if it is an original work. (para. 3)
5. . . . the process can be very **laborious**. (para. 3)
6. However, experts now have a growing **arsenal** of **forensic** techniques . . . (para. 6)
7. . . . (it) may well make it harder to **pass off** forged works of art. (para. 6)

About you

B **Pair work** Take turns using the words and expressions in Exercise A to say something you have learned about the topic of art forgery.

3 Listening Fakes of art!

A 🔊 CD 4.19 Listen to a radio profile of artist John Myatt. Why is he no ordinary artist?

B 🔊 CD 4.20 Listen again. Complete the sentences in no more than four words.

1. A collection of John Myatt's watercolors sold out in _____ months.
2. The story of John Myatt's life is a case of truth being _____.
3. Myatt co-wrote a song _____ called "Silly Games," which was a hit.
4. When his wife left, he had _____ to support.
5. Soon after, he put an ad in a magazine offering to paint _____.
6. An auction house sold one of his paintings for _____ dollars.
7. He went to prison for _____.
8. A police investigator persuaded Myatt to _____ again.

About you

C What do you think of Myatt's story? Should he have been given a longer sentence?

Writing *So what if it's fake?*

In this lesson, you . . .
- report other people's views and give your own.
- use academic conjunctions and adverbs.
- avoid errors with *provided that*.

Task Write an opinion essay.
Producing or selling fake designer goods is illegal. Yet many people buy them. Is it possible to stop these illegal enterprises?

A Look at a model Read the extracts from six essays. Which say that selling fake goods can be stopped (Y)? Which say it can't (N)? Write Y or N. Do you agree with the arguments they make?

1. I would argue that sellers of counterfeit products are unlikely to be stopped irrespective of any efforts to do so given the demand for cheap goods. ____
2. Clearly, people are attracted to fake goods regardless of the economic consequences. Yet if the law were enforced, this industry could be shut down. ____
3. It is inevitable that this activity will continue given that there is a market for fake goods. ____
4. The law can be changed, assuming that there is enough political will to do so. ____
5. I consider buying fake goods to be a form of stealing in view of the fact that it deprives the designers of income. However, it would be naïve to think that it can be stopped. ____
6. This activity can be stopped provided that the authorities take decisive action. ____

B Focus on language Read the chart. Then circle the expressions used in the extracts above.

Conjunctions and adverbs in academic writing

"If": *as long as, assuming (that), provided / providing (that)* ; "But + despite this": *Yet*
This activity can be stopped **as long as** the authorities take decisive action.
Counterfeiting is a serious problem. **Yet** people are attracted to cheap, fake goods.

"Because": *considering (that), in view / light of [the fact (that)], given (that)*
It will continue **in view of the fact / given that** there is a market for fake goods. / **given** the demand.

"Despite": *regardless of, irrespective of, no matter (who / what / how / etc.)*
People buy fake goods **regardless of / irrespective of / no matter** how much it hurts the economy.
  regardless of / irrespective of / no matter what the consequences.

C Complete the sentences with appropriate expressions. There may be more than one answer.

1. People buy fake goods to save money _____ how much harm they are doing to the industry.
2. _____ the time that designers put into creating their work, we should pay the full price.
3. It is illegal to buy counterfeit goods. _____ some people continue to do this.
4. People think it is acceptable to buy fake goods _____ they are for their own personal use.
5. _____ legitimate businesses lose massive profits from the sale of counterfeit products, it is imperative that the law be enforced.

D Write and check Write the essay in the Task above. Then check for errors.

Common errors

Don't use *provided that* to give reasons.
Counterfeit items should not be sold **given that** this is illegal. (NOT *provided that*. . .)

Unit 11: Is it real?

Vocabulary notebook *Use it or lose it.*

Learning tip — **Conversations**

When you learn new words and expressions, put them into a conversation that you can imagine having with a friend.

Friend: Have you read The Hunger Games?
Me: No, but they turned it into a movie, and I saw that.

A Complete the conversations with the expressions from the box. You may need to change the form of the verbs.

| turn back the clock | turn down | turn out | turn over a new leaf | turn to |

1. **A** How was your summer?
   B Actually, it _____ great. It was a little busy, but it was fun.

2. **A** How are things going?
   B Really well. Actually, I've _____ and started going to the gym every day.

3. **A** Did you grow up around your cousins?
   B Yeah. I remember being devastated when we moved away. I wish I could _____ . They were good times.

4. **A** So, are you close to your parents?
   B Oh, yeah. They're the first people I _____ when I need help.

5. **A** You know, I didn't get into college. They _____ my application.
   B Oh, that's too bad. Well, something else is bound to come along.

> **How do we turn?**
> The top collocations with *turn* include *turn out / into / to / around / down / upside down / over / off / up, twists and turns.*

B Use the expressions below to write your own conversations.

| a turning point | turn down | turn your back on |
| turn a blind eye to | turn something around | |

C **Word builder** Find the meanings of these expressions. Then write a conversation using each one.

| turn inside out | turn into | turn upside down | turn up somewhere |

D **Focus on vocabulary** Complete the paragraph with the words in the box. Refer to Exercise 2A on page 123 to help you.

| arsenal | forensic | lucrative | taken in |
| come to light | laborious | passing off | tracing |

_____ fake goods as original designer products is a _____ business. While some consumers may be _____ by these products, many buy the goods knowing they are fake. _____ the criminals who make the goods is not always easy. The work is _____ and requires _____ investigations. However, as more of these products _____ , law enforcement is adding to its _____ of tactics to deal with the problem.

Unit 11: Is it real? 125

Unit 12

Psychology

In Unit 12, you . . .

- talk about independence, attraction, and the brain.
- use objects + *-ing* forms after prepositions and verbs.
- use reflexive pronouns and *each other / one another*.
- explore arguments with expressions like *at the same time*.
- use expressions like *to put it mildly* and *to put it bluntly*.

Lesson A *Being independent*

1 Grammar in context

A In what ways should young adults be independent? Tell the class.

B CD 4.21 Listen. What experience did each person have of becoming independent?

BECOMING INDEPENDENT

In psychology, young people between the ages of 17 and 22 are often characterized as experiencing "early adult transition." At this age, they might leave home to attend college, get their first job, or think about starting their own family. It's a time when young people start to separate from their family attachments and become truly independent. We asked readers to tell us about their experiences of becoming independent.

"Actually, I've always been independent. My parents raised me and my brother that way. They always insisted on us making our own decisions. I guess they were big believers in children being responsible for themselves and their own choices. Like I remember us setting off on a trip one time, and it was snowing, and I wouldn't wear a coat. And I was *frozen* and sobbing. And I remember my mom saying, 'It's your own fault.' She's always hated people complaining about things that are their own fault." CHRIS, 24

"Interestingly enough, I didn't find it hard leaving home. I think actually my parents had a much harder time dealing with me becoming independent. But at the time, they encouraged me to leave without me realizing how difficult it was for them. My mom said later that she and my dad dreaded me leaving and hated the thought of them becoming 'empty nesters.' But for me, it was all just a big adventure." LARRY, 22

"I left home with little experience of being independent. I'd always depended on my parents being there and doing everything for me. Leaving home was a big shock to me. I couldn't cook, didn't know how to do laundry. I mean, there's nothing wrong with children relying on their parents. But it's a balance. I wish mine had been more supportive of me doing things by myself." PAULA, 46

About you

C **Pair work** Discuss the questions.

1. What do you think about Chris's mother's philosophy?
2. Do you know any parents that have suffered from becoming "empty nesters"?
3. Why do you think some parents find it hard when their children leave home?
4. Do you think Paula's experience is common?
5. Whose experience is most similar to your own or is most likely to be?

2 Grammar Describing complex situations and events

Figure it out

A Circle the correct options to complete the sentences. Then read the grammar chart.

1. My parents always insisted on **we make / us to make / us making** our own decisions.
2. She hated the thought of **become / them becoming / them to become** empty nesters.
3. I remember my mom **say / saying / to say**, "It's your choice."

Objects + -ing forms after prepositions and verbs

Grammar extra See page 166.

You can put a noun or pronoun between a preposition and an -ing form, or between some verbs and an -ing form. The noun or pronoun is the object of the preposition or verb and the subject of the -ing form.

verb + preposition	They always **insisted on us making** our own decisions.
adjective + preposition	There's nothing **wrong with children relying** on their parents.
noun + preposition	They were big **believers in children being** responsible for themselves.
verb (e.g., love, hate, not mind, recall, remember)	I **remember us setting** off on a trip. My mom and dad **dreaded me leaving**.

Writing vs. Conversation

In formal writing and speaking, possessive determiners are often used before the -ing form.
*They dreaded **my** leaving.*

About you

B Rewrite the underlined parts of the sentences. Use an object and an –ing form. Then ask and answer the questions with a partner.

1. A How independent were you when you were a kid?
   B Very. I remember that my brother took me off to explore the neighborhood. My parents weren't really concerned about the fact that we might get lost or fall or anything.
   C Not at all. My parents were really protective. They couldn't even deal with the fact that we went away for summer camp. I hated the fact that they fretted so much.

2. A Do you think it's good for young children to be independent?
   B Well, I'm a supporter of the idea that kids should learn to be independent at a young age. I didn't mind that my dad told me to get a job when I wanted a new bike. I was only 12, but I did. There's nothing wrong with the idea that kids should have to do things for themselves.
   C Well, I'm not so sure. I'm a big believer in the idea that kids need to be kids. I don't like the thought that they grow up too early. I don't recall that my parents gave us much responsibility. It resulted in the fact that they raised two happy, carefree kids.

3 Listening "Helicopter" parents

A 🔊 CD 4.22 Listen to the conversation between a mother and her college-age son, Mark. What do they both think of "helicopter" (i.e., overprotective) parents? Do they agree?

I DON'T MIND MY MOM BEING CONCERNED, BUT WHY DOES SHE HAVE TO BE SO LITERAL?

B 🔊 CD 4.23 Listen again and complete the sentences.

1. Mark remembers parents storming into class and . . .
2. Mark's mom recalls moms rushing in if kids . . .
3. Mark says his roommate's mom insists on . . .

About you

C Pair work What are your views on helicopter parents? Do you know any?

Unit 12: Psychology 127

Lesson B Love is blind.

1 Vocabulary in context

A 🔊 CD 4.24 Listen to the podcast. What happened to Dr. Epstein? Why is it ironic?

Who are YOU talking to?

Robert Epstein could rightly describe himself as an expert in human relationships. One might even say a leading expert, if being a former editor of *Psychology Today* is anything to **go by**. However, he proved himself to be as vulnerable as the rest of us when it comes to matters of the heart. A cousin **talked him into** trying online dating, and he **picked out** a photo of an attractive young woman on a dating website. She hadn't written much about herself on her profile, but he liked the photo and wrote to introduce himself. She replied, revealed herself to be Russian, and though her English wasn't good, they started getting to know each other through regular email correspondence. Her letters were warm and affectionate, and he felt that they were attracted to each other. Epstein found it odd that she didn't respond to specific questions, in particular to his suggestion that they might meet. Then, after they had been writing to one another for two months, the realization dawned on him. So he wrote a nonsense message of random characters, to which she replied as usual. The reason for her evasive replies suddenly presented itself. It turned out that he had been conversing with a so-called "chatterbot" – software that interacts with humans on the Internet. As he himself put it, he'd been "had." The clues that should have **given "her" away** were all there, but he had failed to **pick up on** them.

One might think oneself immune to such tricks – that one's judgment would be better – but Epstein's story shows that even the smartest people can fool themselves into thinking they are communicating with a real person. Any one of us might **go about** finding our life partner in this way, and Epstein estimates there are thousands of chatterbots on the Web. So in case you think you could never **be taken in** by a chatterbot yourself, think again. History does repeat itself. At least it did in Dr. Epstein's case. Some time later, he was again fooled by a dating site chatterbot. Interestingly enough, instead of keeping it quiet and **putting it behind him**, Epstein used his experiences in his work, **playing down** in interviews and articles the fact that he corresponded with a chatterbot twice. (He is, after all, also an expert in human-computer interaction.)

In the end, it **comes down to** this: No matter how smart we are, we all want to be loved – and love, as they say, is blind.

About you

B Rewrite the underlined phrases with phrasal verbs from the article. You may need to change the verb forms or word order. Which sentences do you agree with? Compare with a partner.

1. If his profession is anything to <u>be considered</u>, this shouldn't have happened to him.
2. He shouldn't have let his cousin <u>persuade him to try</u> online dating.
3. He couldn't have known when he <u>chose</u> the photo that it was a fake.
4. The poor English in the emails should have <u>revealed</u> "her" <u>secret</u> immediately.
5. It's odd that he didn't <u>notice</u> the fact that it wasn't a real person sooner.
6. It's a matter of someone looking for love, and anyone can <u>be fooled</u> by a chatterbot.
7. It could happen to anyone if they know how to <u>do</u> online dating.
8. If it had happened to me, I'd try to <u>stop being upset by it</u>. Or I'd try to <u>make it seem less serious</u>.

Word sort

C Make charts of phrasal verbs like this. Add other verbs you know. Compare with a partner.

Verb = GO	Meaning	Example sentence
go by	consider, judge, take into account	If you go by his experience, . . . If his experience is anything to go by, . . .
go on	happen	He didn't understand at first what was going on.

Vocabulary notebook
See page 135.

128 Unit 12: Psychology

2 Grammar Referring to people and things

Figure it out

A Which of the two options is the meaning given in the article? What would the other option mean? Then read the grammar chart.

1. Epstein wrote to the woman in the photo to introduce **himself** / **him**.
2. If you think you could never be taken in **yourself** / **yourselves**, think again.
3. People fool **one another** / **themselves** that they're communicating with a real person.

Pronouns

Grammar extra See page 167.

Use reflexive pronouns when the subject and object of a sentence refer to the same person or thing.
*He could rightly describe **himself** as an expert in human relationships.*
*She hadn't written much about **herself** on her profile.*
*One might think **oneself** immune to such tricks, but history often repeats **itself**.*

Reflexive pronouns can also be used for emphasis.
*As he **himself** put it, he'd been "had."*

Use *each other* or *one another* when the subject does something to an object and the object does the same thing to the subject.
*They wrote to **each other** / **one another** for months.*

Common errors

Don't confuse *each other* with *themselves, ourselves, yourselves*.
Helen and I looked at **each other**.
= She looked at me and I looked at her.
We looked at **ourselves** in the mirror.
= I looked at my reflection. She looked at hers.

B Complete the conversation with appropriate pronouns.

A Have you ever been taken in by someone?

B Not that I can think of. But did you ever see that movie *Catfish*? It's about this guy and someone he met online. They wrote to _____ for months. And she'd described _____ as this young woman and sent him these songs that she said she'd written. And he kind of convinced _____ that he was really attracted to her.

A Oh, I've heard those stories, where people fall in love online and then when they meet, they find _____ in this awkward situation where they don't really like _____ at all.

B I know. See, I don't think I'd ever let _____ get into a situation like that. But anyway, he started picking up on these weird things, like that she hadn't written the songs _____. And even though they'd seen photos of _____ and spoken to _____, he realized something wasn't right. So he talked _____ into driving across the country to meet her. Anyway, I don't want to spoil the ending! You'll have to see the movie _____. I guess the story _____ isn't that unusual, but it was interesting that they were able to document it.

3 Viewpoint It's easy to be taken in . . .

Group work Discuss the questions.

- What are some ways that people get taken in by others online?
- Can you get to know someone online? Is it the same as meeting face-to-face?
- How can people protect themselves from situations like the ones in the lesson?
- Do you consider yourself an expert on relationships?
- Do you know anyone who falls in love easily?

"People get taken in by those lottery emails. I got one myself last week, as a matter of fact."

In conversation . . .
You can use *As a matter of fact* to give new or surprising information.

Speaking naturally
See page 143.

Unit 12: Psychology   129

Lesson C *I can see it from both sides.*

1 Conversation strategy Exploring arguments

A Do you ever judge people by their appearance? How do you form an impression of someone?

B ◆)) CD 4.25 Listen. What does Sydney think about judging people by their appearance? How about Nate?

Sydney We were talking in class today about how much appearance matters in society.

Nate Yeah?

Sydney Yeah. Apparently, they say that more attractive people do better in job interviews, and they earn more. I mean, it seems unfair – to put it mildly – that the good-looking ones are more likely to get hired and promoted.

Nate Well, I suppose if you look at it from an employer's perspective, the people who make an effort to look good are probably the ones who make more of an effort at work.

Sydney Possibly. But at the same time, surely your skills and education are more important than how you look.

Nate True. They always say, "Never judge a book by its cover." But equally, shouldn't we try to make ourselves look as good as we can?

Sydney I suppose. But to put it bluntly, there's something not right about employers only hiring people that are attractive.

C **Notice** how Sydney and Nate use expressions like these to consider different aspects of an argument. Find examples in the conversation.

> Considering different points of view:
> *I can see it from both sides.*
> *If you look at it from someone's point of view / perspective, . . .*
>
> Giving different information with the same significance:
> *at the same time, by the same token, equally*

D ◆)) CD 4.26 Read Speaker A's views below. Then listen and complete the various responses. Which views, if any, do you agree with? Discuss the ideas with a partner.

1. A They say you're more likely to stop and help attractive people on the street. That's awful, really.
   B Yeah, but _____ people probably don't do it deliberately. It's probably just instinct.
   C Actually, _____ , you might not feel *safe* stopping and helping a stranger.
   D I guess _____ . I think we're all probably influenced by looks in some way.

2. A You should always trust your first instinct about someone, don't you think?
   B Well, it depends. I mean, instincts can be right. But _____ , sometimes you need time to get to know someone new. Like, I don't like it when people think I'm unfriendly because I'm shy. _____ , I guess I prefer people who are more friendly than I am.
   C Well, _____ . Trust your instincts *and* give people the benefit of the doubt.
   D Yeah. I mean, what if you just met them on a bad day? You should either trust your instincts and hope you're right, or _____ , you can be cautious and let them prove you wrong.

Unit 12: Psychology

2 Strategy plus *To put it mildly*

🔊 CD 4.27 You can use **to put it mildly** to show that you could say something in a stronger or more extreme way.

I mean, it seems unfair – **to put it mildly** – that . . .

When you want to be very direct about what you say, you can use **to put it bluntly**.

But **to put it bluntly**, there's something not right about it.

In conversation . . .
Other expressions are *to put it simply / politely / crudely.*

About you Match the two parts of each comment. Write the letters a–e. Then discuss the views with a partner. Do you agree?

1. They often say people choose a life partner who looks like them. ____
2. People are often suspicious of people who look and dress differently. ____
3. TV is responsible for our obsession with looks. ____
4. People should make an effort to look good. ____
5. Some people care too much about their appearance. ____

a. Though that seems like the last reason to marry someone, to put it mildly.
b. To put it simply, the media just creates unrealistic expectations.
c. To put it bluntly, they should be more concerned with their personality.
d. I mean, to put it bluntly, there's nothing worse than people looking like a mess.
e. Which is pretty shallow, to put it politely. I personally think it makes people interesting.

3 Strategies Stereotypes

A 🔊 CD 4.28 Read the information. Circle the best expressions in the people's reactions. Then listen and check.

1. *Researchers say certain names on résumés receive more callbacks than other names.*
   Mindy   That seems ridiculous, **to put it mildly / equally**. Why should a name matter?
   Leo   Actually, people probably react to names all the time. I mean, **at the same time / to put it bluntly**, they might draw conclusions, for example, about a guy with a feminine name like Lee.
   Harriet   Well, **I can see it from both sides / by the same token**. Either those interviewers are stereotyping people, or maybe it's that they really don't think the person is suitable for the job.

2. *Employers often consider elderly people as less productive and are therefore less likely to employ them.*
   Yvette   That's not fair. I mean, older people have a wealth of experience to contribute. **At the same time / To put it mildly**, it's true they might not be able to do physically demanding work.
   Grant   Well, **I can see it from both sides / if you look at it from an employer's perspective**, I think it's justified because, um, older people are more likely to have health issues. **To put it simply / Equally**, they're more likely to get sick.
   Susan   Well, **I can see it from both sides / to put it bluntly**: Older people may cost a company more, but they're probably reliable.

About you **B** **Pair work** Discuss the information and views in Exercise A. Do you agree? What other stereotypes do people have? Are stereotypes ever justified?

"I have to say it seems unfair, to put it mildly, to judge someone by a name. After all, you don't choose your name."

Unit 12: Psychology 131

Lesson D *Brain matters*

1 Reading

A **Prepare** Which statements do you think are true? What do we know about the brain?

1. Scientists have a clear understanding of the brain.
2. The brains of men and women are different.
3. Brains don't fully develop until the age of 12.
4. Girls are better at language than boys.

B **Read for main ideas** Read the article. Were your guesses in Exercise A correct? How is the brain different across gender and age?

THE DEVELOPING BRAIN

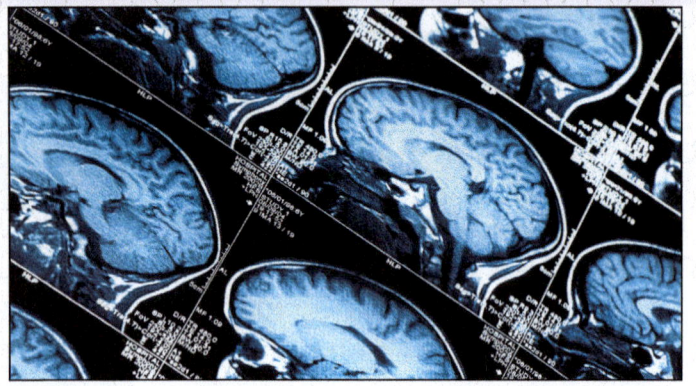

1 At the heart of psychology is understanding behavior, and understanding behavior has much to do with understanding the brain, an endeavor that has proved somewhat elusive. However, as neuroscientists become more efficient at mapping the brain, and as they gain more insight into how the brain develops and functions, scientists believe they may be closer than ever to an understanding of why we behave in the way we do. Differences in behavior as we age and between genders may well be accounted for by the physical state of and changes in our brains.

2 At the age of six, the brain is about 95 percent of its adult size. Over the coming years, it continues to thicken and develop extra connections. Around the age of 12, it is believed that the areas of the brain that are used most will strengthen in terms of neural connectivity. Cells in the brain that are not used tend to wither and die. The implications are enormous. What you do with your brain in your teen years may well determine how your brain functions for the remainder of your life. If a teen spends endless hours watching TV, the neural connections that help the brain process TV are what will strengthen. It is clear, therefore, that how young people spend their time really is of great importance.

3 Surprisingly, and contrary to earlier beliefs, the brain is still developing even in the early twenties. Areas of the brain that are related to emotion, decision making, reasoning, and problem solving are still not fully matured. This may go some way toward explaining impulsive behavior in teens and why vehicular accident rates in young people are significantly higher than those among older people. Young people just don't have the capacity, that is, the set of skills necessary, to make complex judgments while driving.

4 There are also differences in the way brains develop across gender. It appears that girls are ready to process more challenging information earlier than boys, with the area of the brain responsible for this activity peaking at the age of 14 to 16 in boys, a full two years later than girls. In addition, studies have demonstrated that girls and boys process language input in different parts of their brains. Girls typically tend to display stronger language skills than boys. Girls have more brain matter dedicated to language skills. "If there's more area dedicated to a set of skills, it follows that the skills will be more refined," says David Geary, PhD, professor of psychological sciences at the University of Missouri.

5 This kind of research raises important questions about how boys and girls should be taught in schools to maximize their learning. For example, the idea of single-sex education should perhaps be taken into consideration. Experts say that we would do well to revisit the timing of the subjects taught in school, given that some parts of the brain develop before others. Additionally, what we understand about the adolescent brain should perhaps inform public policy and the laws we make with regard to the minimum driving age.

C **Read for detail** Complete the sentences. Then compare with a partner.

1. Mapping the brain is important because _____.
2. How your adult brain works may largely be a result of _____.
3. In their early twenties, young people probably still don't have the skills to _____.
4. The brains of young girls and boys differ in that _____.
5. Understanding the brain may have a social impact – for example, in areas of _____.

D Paraphrase Read the sentences below. Underline the sentences in the article that they paraphrase.

1. After the age of six, the brain continues to mature.
2. How you use your brain as a youngster may well impact the efficiency of your brain as an adult.
3. The brain is still not fully grown in early adulthood, which is the opposite of what was previously believed.
4. Male and female brains mature differently.
5. It is worth thinking about educating male and female students in different schools.

2 Focus on vocabulary *be, do, go, have, take*

A Find the expressions in the box below in the article on page 132. What do they mean? Rewrite the questions using the expressions. Change the forms of the verbs if necessary.

be at the heart of	be of great importance	have to do with	would do well to
be close to	go some way toward	take into consideration	

1. Do you think how we behave **relates to** how our brains are hardwired at birth?
2. What do you think **is the key to** understanding how people behave? Do you think we **are near** an understanding?
3. Do you think lawmakers **should** reconsider the legal age for driving as a result of this research?
4. What aspects of the teenage brain and behavior should schools **think about**?
5. Do you believe that understanding the teenage brain **is essential**? Why?
6. Do you feel the article **gives part of** an explanation of why teens behave differently from adults?

About you

B Pair work Ask and answer the questions in Exercise A.

3 Listening *Understanding the brain — outcomes*

A 🔊 CD 4.29 Listen to four experts lecture about brain research and how it impacts their areas of expertise. Choose the most likely profession of each speaker. Circle a, b, or c.

1. a. education consultant   b. management consultant   c. IT consultant
2. a. marketing consultant   b. chef   c. psychologist
3. a. education consultant   b. mathematician   c. management consultant
4. a. psychiatrist   b. education consultant   c. specialist in aging

B 🔊 CD 4.30 Listen again. How will research impact these areas in the future according to the experts? Complete the notes using as many words as you need.

Lecture 1: What is the research certain to affect?

Lecture 2: What are we coming closer to understanding?

Lecture 3: What may we be able to design in the future?

Lecture 4: What will be easier to treat in the future?

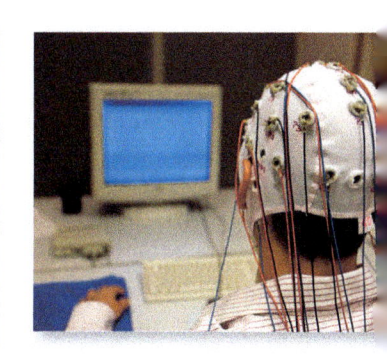

About you

C Pair work Discuss the impact of the research in the different fields mentioned. Which field do you think would benefit most from research? In what ways?

Writing *Twice as likely*

In this lesson, you . . .
- discuss statistics.
- make statistical comparisons.
- avoid errors with *twice*.

Task Write a report with a recommendation.
Write a report on safety issues for a social studies class, and make some recommendations for state policy. Use at least one statistic to support your argument.

A Look at a model Which of the sentences do you think are true? Then read the report and check.

a. Girls use phones more than boys while driving.
b. Girls are less likely to eat while driving than boys.
c. Boys talk to people outside the vehicle more.
d. Boys are less likely to turn around while driving.

Per mile driven, teen drivers have four times as many crashes as adult drivers.* According to research by the AAA Foundation for Traffic Safety, teen girls are . . .
- twice as likely as teen boys to use a cell phone while driving.
- nearly 50 percent more likely than males to reach for an object in the vehicle.
- nearly 25 percent more likely to eat or drink while driving.

The same report shows that teen boys . . .
- are roughly twice as likely as girls to turn around in their seats while driving.
- communicate with people outside of the vehicle twice as often.

*Centers for Disease Control

B Focus on language Read the chart. Then underline the statistical comparisons in Exercise A.

Statistical comparisons in writing

You can make comparisons with adjectives, adverbs, nouns, or pronouns.
Girls are **twice as likely as** boys to use a cell phone.
Teens are **four times more likely** to have a crash **than** adults.
    OR   **as likely** to have a crash **as** adults.
Boys communicate with people outside of the car **twice as often / much**.
Teen drivers have **four times as many** crashes **as** adults. OR **four times more** crashes **than** adults.
    OR   **four times the number of crashes** that adults do.
The cost of insurance for teens can be **five times as much as** for adults.

Writing vs. Conversation

You can use *more* or *as* in phrases like *six times more / as likely*. *More* is more frequent than *as*. *As* is more frequent in writing than in conversation.

C Complete the sentences with the information given. Then write the report in the task above.

1. Sixteen-year-old drivers are _____ to be in a fatal crash when there are three or more young passengers in the car _____ when they are driving alone. (four times / likely)
2. A 16-year-old is only _____ to be involved in a fatal crash with one young passenger in the car. (3% / likely) However, a 17-year-old driver is _____ be involved in a fatal crash. (66% / likely)
3. With an adult passenger over 35, teen drivers are _____ when they are alone. (twice / safe)
4. Boys turn around in their seats while driving _____ girls. (twice / times)
5. Girls use a cell phone while driving _____ boys. (twice / often)
6. If there is loud talk, teen drivers are _____ to have a serious incident. (six times / likely)
7. Insurance costs for a 16-year-old driver can be _____ for an 18-year-old. (twice / much)

D Write and check Write the report in the Task above. Then check for errors.

Common errors

Don't use *twice* + a comparative adjective.
They are **twice as safe** with an adult. (NOT They are ~~twice safer~~ . . .)

Unit 12: Psychology

Vocabulary notebook *Pick and choose*

Learning tip **Thesaurus**

In writing, you often need to refer to the same idea more than once, so it's a good idea to learn different ways to express the same meaning. Create your own thesaurus.

pick out, choose, select, decide on
If I were asked to pick out one book from my favorite author, I would choose The Handmaid's Tale.

A Replace the bold expression in each essay extract to avoid the repetition. Use a word or an expression in the box, and make any other necessary changes.

be a matter of	minimize	persuade	proceed	show their true feelings

1. Charismatic individuals can often **talk** other people **into doing** things they don't want to do. It can be difficult to resist someone who is good at talking people into things.
2. Some people are good at hiding how they feel and not giving anything away. Their expressions do not **give them away**.
3. Many people would like to find the right partner but do not know how to **go about it**. For example, they don't know how to go about finding places to meet people.
4. When it comes down to finding a partner, it is not always easy to make the best choice. Also when it **comes down to** deciding whether or not to get married, you need to be sure.
5. It is important to play down your shortcomings and **play down** your failures in job interviews.

Dictionary tip

Some expressions are too informal for writing. Check in a dictionary. If it says "spoken" or "informal," don't use the expression in formal writing.

hit it off
INFORMAL
to like someone and become friendly immediately

B Match the expressions in bold with the words and expressions on the right. Write the letters a–d. Then rewrite the sentences using the alternatives.

1. It's not always easy to **pick up on** other people's moods. ____
2. If you only **go by** looks, you may choose the wrong partner. ____
3. It's easy to **be taken in** by people who seem sincere. ____
4. You have to **put** difficult or unpleasant experiences **behind you**. ____

a. stop being upset by
b. be fooled
c. take into consideration
d. notice

C **Word builder** Find the meaning of the expressions in bold, and write a word or expression with a similar meaning. Which are too informal for writing?

1. It may be necessary to **brush off** criticism. _____
2. Life can **get to** people sometimes. _____
3. Some people never **hit it off**. _____
4. Often it is better to **give in**. _____

D **Focus on vocabulary** Match the expressions on the left with the ones on the right. Write the letters a–f. (See Exercise 2A on page 133 to help you.)

1. be at the heart of ____
2. have to do with ____
3. be close to ____
4. be of (great) importance ____
5. go some way toward ____
6. would do well to ____

a. be near
b. be essential
c. should, be advised to
d. relate to
e. be the key to
f. help, make progress with

Unit 12: Psychology   135

Checkpoint 4 Units 10–12

1 Change in the workplace

A Change the underlined verbs to continuous forms. Then complete the sentences with reflexive pronouns. One blank needs *each other* or *one another*.

                           be undergoing

Economists say that society will <u>undergo</u> some critical changes in the near future, especially in the workplace. Women seem <u>to graduate</u> in larger numbers than men, although they appear <u>not to take</u> as many graduate courses in science, business, and engineering. Women also appear <u>to have gained</u> momentum in the workplace _____ . They are said <u>to gain</u> in confidence, according to a study by N. Scott Taylor of the University of New Mexico, and now rate _____ as equal to men in terms of leadership qualities. Ask any young professional woman today if she can see _____ in a top job in 15 years from now, and she'll likely say yes. Given that employers will <u>need</u> a more highly educated workforce, it's likely that we are going to see more women in top jobs. What's more, an increasing number of women might well <u>earn</u> more than their spouses. A man who sees _____ as a "traditional" male partner and thinks he ought <u>to earn</u> more than his partner is more likely to feel the relationship _____ is not satisfactory. However, men with "progressive" attitudes are more likely to have high-quality relationships, where respect for _____ is more important than income.

B **Pair work** Discuss the information in Exercise A. Highlight the topics you talk about.

"It's interesting, more women are graduating from college. I wonder why that is?"

2 Pick out the real problem.

A Add a word to each bold expression. Then complete the sentences using the verbs given. Some need passive verbs.

1. **Q:** Would you **turn** <u>turn</u> **your back** on an old friend if she <u>were to do</u> (be to / do) something really bad? A friend of mine was recently arrested for stealing from her employer. She _____ (be to / go) to court next month. She's trying to _____ **it down**, but when it **comes** _____ **to it**, I don't want to **be** _____ **in** by someone who's dishonest.

   A: If your friendship _____ , (be to /continue), then your friend should face up to what she's done. You can't **turn back the** _____, but anyone can **turn over a new** _____ and **turn their** _____ **around**. Tell your friend how you feel. She may appreciate having someone to **turn** _____. Then try to **put it** _____ **you**.

2. **Q:** A friend is trying to **talk me** _____ setting up a business with her. I don't want to **turn the offer** _____ , but I'm not sure. She spends a lot of money and I don't. I know I won't be able **to turn a** _____ **eye to** that. I don't know how to _____ **about** telling her. She's beginning to **pick** _____ **on** my reluctance, though.

   A: This is a common problem, **if my inbox is anything to** _____ **by**. It could **turn** _____ to be a success, or it could **turn** _____ a nightmare. If we _____ (be to / believe) the statistics, many new businesses fail in their first year. Therefore, you are right to be cautious. Maybe you've reached a **turning** _____ **in your lives** and friendship. Your email **gives** _____ one thing – you have different attitudes toward money. You need to talk. Otherwise, it _____ (be bound to / end) in failure.

B **Pair work** Discuss the problems and solutions above. Use expressions like *to me, I can see it from both sides,* and *at the same time* to express different points of view.

Checkpoint 4: Units 10–12

3 A true story

A Complete the story using the verbs given. Many have passive verb complements.

Maybe every young person <u>wants to be known</u> (want / know) as a hero, but very few people get the opportunity. As he left for work one morning, pilot Chesley Sullenberger probably _____ (not expect / call) a national hero later that day. Passengers on Flight 1549 _____ (recall / terrify) as their plane headed into the Hudson River. A flock of geese _____ (appear / suck) into the plane's engine. Sullenberger landed the plane safely on the water. He also made sure that every passenger and crew member was safely out of the plane before leaving the aircraft himself. For this above all, perhaps, he _____ (deserve / admire). It was an incident that many passengers no doubt _____ (would rather / forget). However, it is a feat that the industry _____ (need / remember) for many years to come.

B Pair work Retell this comment on the story. Use *that* and *those* to refer to ideas your partner knows and *this* and *these* to introduce or highlight ideas. Add *to put it mildly* in two more places.

       those   to put it mildly

"I'm sure ~~the~~ passengers were pleased when the plane landed safely. The geese caused a few problems. Just think what could have happened if the pilot hadn't been so skilled. The guy must have nerves of steel. He must have analyzed the problem instantly to bring the aircraft down safely. Then he made sure all the people were safe. I read a story recently about a pilot who fell asleep, which is scary, and some passengers woke him up."

4 In the news?

A Replace the underlined words in the reports with expressions from Unit 10, Lesson A. Then complete the verb phrases to express the ideas given in brackets [ ].

                 greet a delegation

1. The failure of the president to <u>meet a group</u> of foreign heads of state this week has <u>encouraged rumors</u> about the state of her health. She <u>had surgery</u> earlier this year. However, it is thought that doctors are insisting **on** <u>her having</u> [= *insisting that she should have*] more surgery before they can **agree to** _____ [= *agree that she can carry out*] her normal duties. This comes in a week when her main political rival <u>stated he was running for office</u>. Analysts say with the political uncertainty, there is **a danger of** _____ [= *that the stock market be affected*]. They say they cannot <u>exclude the idea</u> **of** _____ [= *idea that the economy may collapse*]. Stocks <u>fell sharply</u>.

2. A bomb <u>exploded</u> near a central market in the capital early this morning. There were no injuries. A protest group has said it <u>was responsible</u>. If these protests continue, it could result **in** _____ [= *have the result that the government will take action*]. Riot squads may be <u>put on the streets</u>. A government spokesperson said that victims will be <u>paid damages</u> and that the protest movements need to be <u>controlled</u>. It is thought the government is already <u>preparing a legal case</u> against one group.

B Complete the sentences from an editorial column with an appropriate verb in the subjunctive.

1. The requirement that every student _____ an advanced English exam to graduate is a good one.
2. It is essential that everyone _____ English well.
3. Our recommendation is that English exams _____ harder.
4. Colleges should demand that any student who fails _____ in college for another year.
5. It is crucial that our country _____ better at English than neighboring countries.

C Pair work Do you agree with the editorial in Exercise B? What subjects do you think should be mandatory? Signal your concerns with expressions like *That doesn't sit right with me*.

Checkpoint 4: Units 10–12

Speaking naturally

Unit 7, Lesson B Binomial pairs

Notice how *and* and *but* are reduced in these binomial expressions. Notice also that the primary stress is on the second word of the pair and the secondary stress on the first.

I'm **sick and tired** of getting work calls at night. When I'm home, I need **peace and quiet**.

I suspect that, **slowly but surely**, phone calls will become an issue between me and my wife.

A Read and listen to the information above. Repeat the example sentences.

B Read the conversation. Circle the bold words that have the primary stress. Underline the bold words with secondary stress. Then listen, check, and repeat.

A Guess what! I just quit my job. I gave notice on Friday.
B Really? I thought you were going to **wait and see** if things got better.
A Yeah, but you know, **slowly but surely**, things were getting worse, so . . .
B Well, you and your boss certainly had your **ups and downs**.
A That's for sure. I mean, I went **above and beyond** most of the other staff, and he'd still criticize me. I just got **sick and tired** of it.
B Yeah. But did you **stop and think** what you might do? I mean, now you have no job to go to.
A Well, actually, I might do a PhD now that I have the **time and energy**!

About you **C Pair work** Practice the conversation. Then discuss the situation. Did Speaker A do the right thing? Why, or why not?

Unit 8, Lesson A Saying perfect infinitives

Notice that in perfect infinitives, *to* is not reduced, but *have* is reduced.

My grandfather seems **to have had** an extremely interesting career as a journalist.
I'd like **to have known** him, but he died before I was born.
I'd like **to have spoken** to him about his experiences in war zones.

A Read and listen to the information above. Repeat the example sentences.

B Listen and repeat these sentences. Pay attention to the pronunciation of the perfect infinitives.

1. I'd like **to have studied** math with Einstein. He's said **to have been** a great teacher.
2. I would love **to have gone** to the moon with Neil Armstrong.
3. People seem **to have lived** much simpler lives 100 years ago – certainly less stressful.
4. My grandparents' generation seems **to have had** more time to spend with family.
5. We're supposed **to have made** great progress in how we handle conflict, but I'm not so sure.
6. People are said **to have lived** healthier lives until about 20 years ago.

About you **C Pair work** Discuss the sentences. Do you agree?

Speaking naturally

Speaking naturally

Unit 9, Lesson C   Intonation of background information

> Expressions that give background information, or information you expect your listener to know, have a fall–rise intonation: *considering . . ., given (that / the fact that) . . ., in view of (the fact that) . . ., in light of (the fact that). . . .*
>
> Space exploration is expensive. **Considering the cost**, it makes no sense at all to go to Mars.
>
> It makes no sense at all to go to Mars, **considering the cost**.

A 🔽 Read and listen to the information above. Repeat the example sentences.

B 🔽 Listen to this conversation. Circle the stressed words where the fall-rise intonation starts in the underlined parts of the sentences.

   A I'm getting worried about the storms we've had recently, <u>given all the (damage).</u>
   B Well, <u>in light of rising sea levels</u>, I think this is just the beginning. Frankly, I think it's time for people to start moving away from the coasts.
   A Maybe. But what are we going to do about places like New York, Bangkok, and Rio? We can't just move entire cities, <u>given the huge populations.</u>
   B No, but we could build sea walls for protection, <u>given how serious this is.</u>
   A I don't think that's going to happen anytime soon, <u>considering the incredible cost.</u>
   B But <u>in view of the fact that 15 of the world's 20 largest cities are in flood zones</u>, we can't ignore the problem. We have to find ways to protect the people in these cities.

About you   **C**   *Pair work*   Practice the conversation. Which ideas do you agree with?

Unit 10, Lesson C   Stress and intonation

> Notice how longer sentences can be broken up into parts. Each part has a primary stress, where the intonation changes, and often a secondary stress as well. Notice also the fall–rise intonation for background information and falling intonation for new information.
>
> My **girl**friend, / she's **al**ways **watch**ing / those **cook**ing **shows**.
> [Background]   [New]   [New]

A 🔽 Read and listen to the information above. Repeat the example sentences.

B 🔽 Each phrase has two stressed syllables shown in bold. Listen and circle the syllable with the primary stress.

   1. Those **shop**ping **chan**nels, / I **nev**er **watch** them. / **They** can be ad**dic**tive.
   2. This **friend** of **mine**, / he's **al**ways on his **smart**phone, / **check**ing the **finan**cial news.
   3. The **weath**er **chan**nels, / now **they're useful**. / The **weath**er re**ports** / are **con**stantly **up**dated.
   4. The **cook**ing **chan**nels, / **they're** a **lot** of fun. / You can **learn** to **cook** / **sim**ply by **watch**ing them.
   5. My **moth**er and **fath**er, / they **leave** the TV on / pretty **much** all **day**. / I **guess** they **like** it / when there's **back**ground **noise**.

About you   **C**   *Pair work*   Rewrite each comment with your own information. Discuss with your partner.

Speaking naturally

Unit 11, Lesson B Stress in longer idioms

Phrasal verbs are usually stressed on the particle. However, in idioms that are phrasal verbs with a noun object, the object has the primary stress.

I **turned around** and looked in the mirror.

I realized that I needed to **turn my life around**. BUT I **turned it around**.

A Read and listen to the information above. Repeat the example sentences.

B Listen. Circle the word that has the primary stress in the bold expressions. Then listen, check, and repeat.

1. Have you ever known anyone who was in a bad situation but was able to **turn his life around**?
2. Have you ever needed to **turn your back on** friends who were doing things you didn't approve of?
3. If you knew some friends were cheating on exams, would you **turn a blind eye to** what they were doing? Or would you **turn them in** to the teacher?
4. Have you ever wanted to **turn over a new leaf** for any reason?
5. Do you ever feel you want to **turn back the clock** to a time when life was more fun?
6. Have you ever regretted **turning down an opportunity** of some kind?

About you **C** *Pair work* Take turns asking and answering the questions.

Unit 12, Lesson B Stress with reflexive pronouns

Notice how reflexive pronouns are stressed when they are used for emphasis. They are generally unstressed in other cases.

*Once my parents found **themselves** in trouble because some harassing emails had been sent from their computer. They **themselves** hadn't sent the messages, of course.*

*I **myself** have never had a problem with my email. But once I let **myself** be tricked into giving money to a con artist on the street.*

A Read and listen to the information above. Repeat the example sentences.

B Listen. Circle the stressed reflexive pronouns. Then listen, check, and repeat.

1. People allow **themselves** to taken in by the same scams again and again. If you think you'll never get taken in **yourself**, think again. History repeats **itself**.
2. I wouldn't describe **myself** as terribly cautious, but I never open emails if I don't recognize the sender. I've never had a virus **myself**, but I just want to protect **myself**.
3. You have to be careful not to let **yourself** be fooled when you meet people online. They often say things about **themselves** that are simply untrue.
4. My brother got so upset with **himself** because he was spending too much time on social media, so he deleted all his accounts. It was a decision he made **himself**.

About you **C** *Pair work* Read the comments aloud. What do you think of the ideas they express?

Unit 7, Lesson A
More on inversions

Grammar extra

- Inversions are generally used in formal English. Use *were* + subject (+ infinitive) to describe an imaginary situation in the present or future. Use *had* + subject + past participle for the past.
  Were he to have a child, my son would take classes.   Negative: *Were he **not** to have ...*
  Had they known about the classes, my friends would have   Negative: *Had they **not** known ...*
  taken them.

- You can also use *If it weren't for . . ., If it hadn't been for . . ., Were it not for . . .,* and *Had it not been for* + noun phrase. They mean "If someone or something didn't exist or something hadn't happened."
  If it weren't for *my parents, I wouldn't be able to continue with my education.*
  OR ***Were it not for*** *my parents, I . . .* (hypothetical statement about the present)
  If it hadn't been for *my parents, I wouldn't have been able to continue with my education.*
  OR ***Had it not been for*** *my parents, I . . .* (hypothetical statement about the past)

A Rewrite the underlined parts of the blog about parenting teenagers, using a structure in the chart. Start with the word in bold.

There are many challenges associated with parenting, especially parenting teens. Some parents claim that **if** the advice in parenting magazines didn't exist, they would not know how to deal with their teenage children. If these magazines **had** existed when we were younger, we could certainly have learned from them. We relied instead on our friends for advice. Indeed, if my wife and I **had** not had the support of other parents with the same challenges, we may not have survived the journey. **If** our neighbor in particular hadn't existed, life would have been much harder. We had it tough, or so we thought. However, as you get older, you realize your "mistakes." If we **had** been able to see things from our teenager's perspective, we may have realized that it was our daughter who needed the advice – on how to handle us, her parents. Now a parent herself, she discussed this with us recently. If she **had** not done so, we may not have formed the close bond that we have today. She said:

1. If I **were** suddenly to find myself a parent of teenagers, I'd trust them to make good decisions.
2. If I **had** thought you would listen without judging me, I would have talked to you more openly.
3. If it **were**n't for the fact that you were always so busy, I would have spent more time with you.

If it **had**n't been for that conversation, we would probably have interfered too much as grandparents, too. Now we trust her decisions as a new parent. If she **were** a teenager today, our daughter would be proud of us!

B Complete the company article extracts about its family-friendly policies. Use the words given and a structure from the chart.

All parents complained of high childcare costs before our childcare center opened 10 years ago. Many say that _____ (it / not be) for their own parents' help, they could not have continued to work when their children were small. The center is highly valued by employees. "_____ (it / not be) for the care center, I simply couldn't do this job," is a typical comment. The costs of running this facility are high, but _____ (be) the center _____ (close), the company would lose experienced employees. Flexible working is also important. Most parents said that _____ (they / have) the opportunity to work part-time when their children were small, they would have done so. Others said they needed two incomes. One told us, "_____ (we / not keep) working, we couldn't have managed financially." Trying to juggle family life and career is still an issue. Many non-parents report that _____ (it / not be) for their careers, they might start families earlier.

Unit 7, Lesson B — Grammar extra

1 More on *what* clauses

- Speakers often use a *what* clause as the subject of a verb to do the things below.

Describe and analyze situations	*What we're seeing is . . . What we do know is . . . What we've seen is . . . What we've found is . . . What's happening now is . . . What it comes / boils down to is . . .*
Say what is being done	*What we're doing is . . . What we've done is . . . What we're (really) trying to do is . . . What we don't want to do is . . .*
Say what is needed or wanted	*What we need to / have to do is . . . What we want to do is . . . What we're looking for is . . . What we would like to do is . . .*

Rewrite the underlined sentences in the article. Use *what* clauses and add the verb *is*.

An organization recently released a report on the state of families today. The report said, "We're seeing today the unprecedented breakdown of relationships." While the cause of the breakdowns is complex, the report emphasized, "We do know that divorce is tearing families apart." Their survey asked people, "How do you keep your relationship strong?" Here are some excerpts from the responses.

1. "We're creating more family time."
2. "My husband and I have gone to counseling."
3. "We want to stay together. We've found that it gets easier with time."
4. "It boils down to being more tolerant of other people."
5. "It comes down to small things, like doing something special for each other every day."

2 *what* clauses with passive verbs and modals in writing

- In some *what* clauses, *what* is the subject of a passive verb.
  What was intended to be a small, quiet wedding became a huge affair.
  There may be a problem if your income falls short of **what is needed** to run your home.

- You can use these phrases in writing to define words and expressions: *what is / are called, what is / are known as, what is / are termed.*
  When planning a wedding, many couples choose **what is known as** a "full wedding package."
  My grandparents had **what is called** an "arranged introduction."

- This is a common pattern with modal verbs in object *what* clauses:
  We are always being told what we **can and cannot** do, what we **should and should not** think.

Complete the article extracts about the "worst marriage trends." Use the words given.

1. In Japan, some couples get _____ (what / know) the "Narita divorce." It's named after the airport near Tokyo and refers to the fact that the couple starts divorce proceedings on returning from their honeymoon.
2. _____ (what / consider) by most people to be a private experience after the wedding – the honeymoon – is becoming a family and friends affair. A group honeymoon, or _____ (what / call) by some a "buddymoon," is the latest "worst trend."
3. An email to four bridesmaids from a bossy bride – or _____ (what / call) a "bridezilla" – has gone viral. The bride told them what they _____ (could / wear) and what they _____ (must / do).
4. In case you're not sure _____ (what / require) to create a cost-effective wedding, it is _____ now _____ (what / term) a "drive through" ceremony. Couples are getting married at fast-food restaurants!

Unit 8, Lesson A — Grammar extra

1 More on perfect infinitives

- You can use perfect infinitives after verbs in the present or past.
  He **seems** **to have fooled** everyone. (= It seems now that he fooled everyone.)
  He **was said** **to have had** special powers. (= It was said in the past that he had special powers.)

- There are three negative forms. The first is the most frequent and the third the least frequent.
  His wealth **does not appear to have changed** him.
  His wealth **appears not to have changed** him.
  His wealth **appears to have not changed** him.

Rewrite the underlined parts in this biography. Change the *it* clauses, using perfect infinitives, and change the punctuation. Sometimes there is more than one correct answer.

Near the end of his life, the great magician Harry Houdini, it was known, *(Harry Houdini was known to have suffered)* suffered from appendicitis, for which, it was said, he refused treatment. However, as part of a challenge, a Canadian student unexpectedly punched him in the stomach, which, it was believed, caused Houdini a fatal injury. It was a sad ending for a man who people still think is the greatest magician of all time. As in death, his life was shrouded in mystery and, it seems, caused great speculation. It was Harry Houdini himself who claimed to be a native of Appleton, Wisconsin. However, he was actually born in Budapest, Hungary, and moved to the U.S. when his family emigrated in 1878. His family, it appears, wasn't wealthy. But the poverty in which he lived, it appeared, did not deter him from seeking success. Houdini, it is known, tried all kinds of magic tricks early in his career. However, his early tricks, it seems, weren't successful. He, it appears, got his biggest break with an act where he freed himself from a pair of handcuffs. It was the start of an extraordinary career as an escape artist.

2 The perfect infinitive after adjectives and nouns

- You can use perfect infinitives after some adjectives and nouns.
  He was **fortunate** **to have escaped**.   It was an **honor** **to have been** there.
  I'm very **lucky** **to have met** her.   It was a terrible **thing** **to have done**.
  I was too **young** **to have understood**.   She was the only **person** **to have achieved** that.

Read the information about Nelson Mandela. Rewrite the underlined parts of the sentences by using the perfect infinitive.

1. Many students today are too young <u>and didn't see</u> Nelson Mandela released from jail in 1990.
2. He is one of many activists <u>who strived</u> for racial equality in South Africa in the 1960s.
3. While he was dismayed <u>when he received</u> a life sentence in prison for his activist work, he remained true to his beliefs for a free and equal society. He spent 27 years in prison.
4. It was a remarkable accomplishment <u>when he came out</u> of jail without any anger or resentment.
5. It was also an achievement <u>that he became</u> president of South Africa in 1994.
6. It must have been an honor <u>hearing</u> his first speech after his release.
7. He is one of only two people <u>that became</u> an honorary citizen of Canada.
8. Many of the celebrities who have visited South Africa say they feel privileged <u>because they met</u> him.
9. I'm sure he was proud <u>that he contributed</u> so much to his country's history.

Unit 8, Lesson B — Grammar extra

1. More on cleft sentences with *it + be*

In cleft sentences with *it + be*, the item that you focus on can be the subject or object of the next clause. When it is the object, you can leave out *who, that,* or *which.*

Subject *The Internet* changed everything in the twentieth century.
→ **It was the Internet that** changed everything in the twentieth century.

Object Martin Cooper invented **the cell phone**.
→ **It was the cell phone (that / which)** Martin Cooper invented.
I remember studying **Edison** for a history project.
→ **It's Edison (who / that)** I remember studying.

Read the story. Rewrite the sentences, using *it + be* clefts to focus on the words in bold.

There were many influential figures in my past, but **my grandpa** influenced me most. When I was still an impressionable child, he took me to the Kennedy Space Center in Florida. I will never forget it as an **adventure.** I remember staring in awe at the space shuttle and riding in the simulators. However, the **exhibit** that explained how NASA needed children like me to become scientists had the biggest impact on me. I realized we have **NASA scientists** to thank for many of the things we see in daily life: baby formula, freeze-dried food, and ear thermometers. Not only that, but **NASA technology** put people into space. That **day** changed everything for me all those years ago. Looking back on my childhood, I recall **those NASA scientists** as being my heroes. Today I'm a scientist, and I told **my grandpa** first about my ambition to become one. **His response** convinced me. "Of course you can be a scientist. You can be anything you want to be," he said.

2. *It + be* + noun phrase in writing

- In writing, some cleft sentences with *it + be* + noun are used to introduce issues, e.g.:
  It is no coincidence that . . ., It is a fact that . . ., It is no accident that . . ., It is no wonder that . . ., It is no surprise that . . ., It is a shame / pity that . . .
  It is no coincidence that countries with strong economies became politically dominant.

- Other expressions refer back to something that has just been mentioned, e.g.:
  It is an issue that . . ., It was a decision that . . ., It is a story that . . ., It is a system/process that . . ., It was a reminder that . . ., It was a moment that . . .
  In 1919, the atom was first split. **It was a moment that** changed history forever.

Complete the sentences in the article. Use *it + be* + the noun phrase given + *that*.

On July 20, 1969, the Apollo 11 spacecraft landed on the moon. <u>It was an event that</u> (an event) will forever be remembered in history, and _____ (no surprise) more than half a billion people watched it on television. During the previous decade, _____ (no coincidence) other countries had been developing rockets of their own. _____ (a period) became known as the "Space Race," as countries competed to develop superior space technologies.

In 1961, a Russian cosmonaut named Yuri Gagarin became the first human to go into space. _____ (a move) spurred President John F. Kennedy to announce a program to land people on the moon by the end of the decade. _____ (a decision) energized the entire nation. However, in 1967, during a launch test, three U.S. astronauts were killed. _____ (a tragedy) almost derailed the whole program. After an overhaul of the entire operation, the Apollo 11 mission was ready. As Neil Armstrong stepped onto the surface of the moon in 1969, he declared, "That's one small step for man, one giant leap for mankind." For those watching, _____ (a day) they will never forget, and for everyone else, _____ (a moment) defined an era.

Unit 9, Lesson A — Grammar extra

1 whatever, whichever, and whoever as subjects and objects

- *Whatever, whichever,* and *whoever* can be the subject or object of a verb.
  - **Subject** **Whatever** happened to the idea of building things to last?
  - **Object** **Whichever (program)** you choose, make sure it's one that you're interested in.

- Sometimes a clause with *whatever, whichever,* or *whoever* is the subject or object of a verb.
  - **Subject** **Whatever happens in your career** is your responsibility.
  - **Object** We don't just take **whoever applies to this program**.

> **Common errors**
> Don't confuse *whatever* and *whether*. *Whether* introduces alternatives.
> **Whether** you are an employer or an employee, come to our job fair. (NOT ~~Whatever you~~ . . .)

Read the report about women in STEM professions. Complete the sentences with *whatever, whichever, whoever,* or *whether*. Sometimes there is more than one correct answer.

1. Researchers found gender bias against women in _____ jobs they chose in the fields of science, technology, engineering, and math – also known as STEM fields.
2. Women are often considered as less capable than men _____ their qualifications are.
3. _____ STEM field they pursued, women were often also seen as less likable than men.
4. High school test scores now show that _____ wants to excel in STEM subjects can do so.
5. If the school environment is right, girls can excel in _____ STEM subject they choose.
6. _____ else high school teachers may do, however, they must focus on teaching spatial skills to girls.
7. Colleges should not just accept _____ applies for STEM majors. They should actively recruit girls into these courses.
8. All students, _____ male or female, should be mentored in college.

2 Patterns with *however* and *whatever*

- *However* can be used before *much / many* and before adjectives and adverbs.
  Engineering is well worth studying, **however many** years it takes, **however much** it costs.
  We will solve the problem, **however complex** (it may be), and **however long** it takes.

- The pattern *whatever the* + noun means "it doesn't matter what the (noun) is."
  We should make efforts to train a new generation of engineers, **whatever the cost**.
  Whatever the reason, engineering isn't attracting as many students as we need.

> **In writing . . .**
> The most common collocations in *whatever the* + noun are *reason(s), case, outcome, cause, merits, explanation, price, cost.*

Rewrite the underlined parts of the comments using *however* or *whatever* + an adjective or adverb, or *whatever the* + noun.

1. <u>It doesn't matter how much you aim to earn in life</u> – and <u>it doesn't matter how</u> hard you try – you won't find a better career than engineering, in my view.
2. Engineering is a good choice, <u>no matter what the cost is</u> and <u>no matter how demanding the course</u>.
3. <u>It doesn't matter what the cause is</u>, there are simply not enough engineers.
4. <u>It doesn't matter how many engineers we train</u>, there will never be enough.
5. <u>It doesn't matter what the financial merits are</u> of a career in engineering, nothing beats the feeling of creating solutions to problems, <u>no matter how challenging they are</u>.

Unit 9, Lesson B — Grammar extra

1 More on inversion

- Use inversion when these adverbs begin a sentence. Notice the words that begin a second clause.

  Negative adverbs: *Not only . . . (but), Never, Nowhere, No sooner . . . than, No longer*
  Adverbs with negative meaning: *Hardly / Scarcely . . . when, Little, Rarely, Seldom*
  Only + adverb, prepositional phrase, or clause: *Only then, Only after, Only when . . .*
  Expressions with *no*: *At no time, At no point, By no means, Under no circumstances*

  Not only does it **wobble** as people walk across it, **(but)** it also causes nausea.
  No sooner had the paint **dried** at one end **than** it needed repainting.
  Hardly had construction **begun when** there were problems.
  It opened. **Only then / Only after the ceremony / Only when it opened did** they **see** the problem.
  At no time did anyone **raise** any objections to the construction of this bridge.

- Do not use inversion after *only*, *hardly*, and *scarcely* when they modify a noun, or after *In no time*.
  Hardly a week went by that there wasn't a problem. **In no time, they built** the main structure.

Rewrite the information, starting with the bold negative adverb or a negative equivalent (e.g., As soon as → No sooner). Use inversions where necessary.

> **In writing. . .**
> After *Nowhere*, there is often a comparison.
> *Nowhere was the need for redevelopment more evident than here.*

There isn't a more famous sight **anywhere in the world** than the Leaning Tower of Pisa. However, its designers did not intend the tower to lean **by any means**. **As soon as** construction started, problems began. Work had **hardly** begun on the tower in 1173 **when** engineers noticed it was leaning. In the following centuries, it **not only** leaned farther, but it also seemed like it would collapse. It was **only after** it became unsafe in the early 1990s that authorities finally closed the tower. And it was **only then** that there was an effort to stabilize it. **As soon as** it closed, work started. A day **hardly** went by that there wasn't a danger of collapse. Nevertheless, the tower was restored. Today, the tower has **not only** reopened to the public, it has been declared safe for 200 years.

2 Inversion with modals and in passive sentences

- After negative adverbs, the inversion with modal verbs is modal + subject + verb.
  Never again would anyone **achieve** anything of this size.

- In simple present and past passive sentences, the inversion is *be* + subject + past participle.
  Under no circumstances is / was this project **allowed** to be delayed.

- In present or past perfect passive sentences, the inversion is *have* + subject + *been* + past participle.
  Never has / had such a large project **been completed** on time.

Unscramble the sentences, starting with the negative adverb.

Hong Kong International Airport at Chek Lap Kok is a remarkable feat of engineering.
1. attempted / nowhere before / been / a more complex airport project / had
2. nowhere in the world / an island / had / constructed / on which to build an airport / been
3. completed / been / had / a project this size / under budget / rarely
4. could / bringing in thousands of workers / only by / the project / be accomplished
5. however, under no circumstances / permitted / the project / to fail / was
6. no sooner / were / finished / than work began / the designs
7. was / not only / completed on time, / but it was finished under budget / the project

Unit 10, Lesson A — Grammar extra

1 Simple vs. continuous infinitives

- Infinitives can be simple or continuous. The simple form describes single or repeated events in a factual way. It can also suggest that an event is complete.
  *A scientist claims **to have found** a cure for malaria. She hopes **to publish** her research soon.*

- The continuous form describes events as activities that are ongoing or temporary. It can suggest that the event is not complete.
  *The team appears **to have been working** on their research for several decades.*
  *They seem **to be making** great progress.*

Complete the infinitives in the editorial with the verbs given. Sometimes both simple and continuous forms are correct.

Weather-forecasting techniques appear to have _____ (improve). Certainly, the predictions of the scale and timing of major weather events, such as hurricanes, seem to have _____ (become) more accurate – fortunately so, because the frequency of strong storms appears to _____ (increase). However, what we, as a society, appear not to _____ (do) is to recognize how serious forecasters' warnings are and take appropriate action. As another huge storm hits the coast, some residents of low-lying areas appear not to have _____ (listen) to the reports on TV and radio that urged them to evacuate. They seem to have _____ (hope) that the forecasts were exaggerated. Others were too poor _____ (move) and seem to have _____ (have) no help from officials. Now, looking at the devastation, many are lucky to have _____ (survive). The whole city appears to have _____ (stop) working even though officials are likely to have _____ (prepare) for a state of emergency for several days and despite the efforts of utility companies, which we believe to _____ (work) around the clock to restore power. They hope to _____ (get) the city back to normal in the next few days. We are fortunate to have _____ (have) the warnings, but many of us are unwise to have _____ (ignore) them.

2 More on perfect continuous infinitives

- Verbs that are followed by perfect continuous infinitives can be present or past, active or passive.
  *The hacker **seems** to have been working alone.*
  *The economy **appeared** to have been growing steadily until 2008.*
  *The government **appears** to have been negotiating secretly with unions on a new pay deal.*
  *A terrorist group **is believed / is alleged** to have been planning attacks for several months.*

Rewrite these news excerpts without using *it* clauses.

Unemployment rates appear to have been declining

1. It appears that unemployment rates have been declining in recent months. However, it is not believed that the economy has been making a sufficient recovery.
2. Twenty soccer fans, who, it was alleged, had been traveling to an international match with the intention of causing a riot, have been arrested and banned from all future European matches.
3. It is said that workers' unions have been talking with employers in the auto industry this week.
4. A man was arrested after disrupting a flight en route to Miami. It is thought the man had been suffering from an anxiety attack.
5. While it appeared that the coal mining industry had been declining in the last part of the twentieth century, it is reported that clean coal technology has been revitalizing the industry.
6. A man who, it was believed, was diving for sunken treasure has been reported missing.

Unit 10, Lesson B — Grammar extra

1 More on the subjunctive

- The subjunctive form is used for both the present and the past. It does not change.
  *An editor may require that a journalist **reveal** his or her sources.*
  *The military instisted that all reporters **leave** the war zone.*

- The negative subjunctive is *not* + verb. Do not use *do / does / did*.
  *It is often advisable that a local journalist **not report** the truth about corrupt officials.*

- Passive forms of the subjunctive are *be* + past participle and *not be* + past participle.
  *It is essential that interviewees **be treated** with respect.*
  *We requested that the exact location of the journalists **not be broadcast**.*

Read the editorial. Find 10 verbs you can change to the subjunctive form, either by deleting a verb or changing the form of a verb.

Journalists who cover combat zones often pay the ultimate price for their determination to report the news. While media outlets may not require a reporter to leave a war zone, they often encourage him or her to do so. Even so, journalists often insist that they should be allowed to stay. Typically, they request that their exact locations are not revealed to ensure their safety. While viewers demand that journalists should provide detailed reporting on conflicts worldwide, it is essential that the dangers they face in doing their work are recognized. One such courageous reporter died this week. Her family asked the media to respect their privacy. However, she herself requested that her work should not be abandoned. Indeed, in a video made shortly before her death, she said that it was critical that the plight of civilians in the cross fire is publicized. This editor asks that this reporter should not be forgotten. It is important that she is remembered for her courage in reporting the truth.

2 The subjunctive and conditional sentences

- The subjunctive can also be used in conditional sentences after *on condition that*.
  *A witness agreed to testify on condition that he **remain** anonymous / he **not be named**.*

- You can use *whether it / they be . . . or . . .* OR *be it / they . . . or . . .* to introduce alternative ideas.
  They mean "whether we are talking about one thing or another, the issue is the same."
  *One way to read the news, **whether it be** print **or** broadcast media, is to question what you read.*
  *The problem with news reporting, **be it** live **or** recorded, is that it is always selective.*

Rewrite the underlined parts of this editorial with *on condition that*, *whether it be*, or *be it* (both may be possible) with the same meaning. Make any other changes necessary.

> **Writing vs. Conversation**
> The subjunctive is rarely used in conversation. However, *whether it / they be . . . or . . .* is more frequent in conversation than in writing.

It makes no difference if it's a television report or a printed news article, bias exists. Research shows 1 in 6 adults perceive bias in the news, both liberal and conservative. Reporting should be balanced, either in terms of reporting a range of perspectives or reflecting the diversity of public opinion. There are other problems with the way in which stories are reported, both in the use of biased language and in the fact that certain stories are given more coverage. One reporter stated, and he insisted that he did not want to be identified, that the media represent the views of the sources of their funding. Media outlets, and the issue is the same if they are transparent or not, show bias, so read as many sources as possible.

Unit 11, Lesson A — Grammar extra

1 More on *be to; be due to, be meant to*

- You can use *be to* to describe fixed events in the future, especially official or scheduled events.
  The president **is to** host a summit of world leaders in May. World leaders **are to** meet in May.

- You can use passive verbs after *be to* expressions.
  Meetings **are to be held** in July, and a report **is to be published** in the fall.
  The government is looking at new technology, which **is about to be tested** in national trials.

- *Be to* can be used in conditional sentences to state what is expected or assumed.
  If we **are to** believe scientists, weather patterns are changing. (= If we are expected to believe)

- *Be due to* suggests that the time is or was known. *Be meant to* means "what is or was intended."
  The report **is not due to** be published until next week. Results **were due to** be announced last week.
  The law **is meant to** protect citizens from cyberattacks. It **was not meant to** restrict freedoms.

Read the article and complete it with the prompts given. Use the passive where necessary.

State officials _____ (due / attend) a national disaster conference next month as part of a series of events. The upcoming conference _____ (be / consider) how to cope with major disasters. "It _____ (mean / teach) us how to survive," the governor stated, "in the event of a major catastrophe." With so many in the media declaring, "The world _____ (about / end)," it would serve us well to know how to survive. But how likely is such an event? The world _____ (due / end) in 2012, but it didn't. In fact, if the media hype _____ (be / believe), disasters would have struck the world several times over in the last decade. Disaster theories have suggested that nuclear weapons _____ (about / launch) accidentally, that millions of people _____ (about / kill) by a deadly virus, or that the northern United States _____ (about / destroy) by a super volcano. While much of the hype _____ (be / ignore), there are other real dangers if experts' warnings _____ (be / believe). Perhaps, then, we really *should* prepare for disaster. If water supplies _____ (be / interrupt), what would you do? If your family _____ (be / force out) of the area, where would you go? If your community _____ (be / hold) a disaster awareness event next month, attend – it could save your life.

2 *be to* for orders and instructions

- *Be to* is used to give or describe orders and instructions, mostly in official notices or written instructions.
  No one **is to use** the fire exits except in an emergency. Staff members **are not to open** windows.
  These doors **are to be kept** closed at all times. They **are not to be left** open.

Read this emergency fire plan from a company website. Rewrite the plan, using *be to*.

1. Keep all fire doors shut at all times. *All fire doors are to be kept shut at all times.*
2. Do not tamper with fire alarms and sprinkler systems.
3. If the fire alarms sound, staff members should leave all personal belongings and exit the building.
4. Staff members should not stay in the building under any circumstances.
5. No one should use the elevators in the event of a fire.
6. All staff members should meet in the parking lot.
7. Each department head should take a roll call once staff is assembled in the parking lot.
8. No one should leave the lot until notified that it is permissible to do so.
9. Under no circumstances should anyone return to the building without notification from the fire department.

Unit 11, Lesson B — Grammar extra

1 More on passive perfect infinitives

> - Passive perfect infinitives can follow active or passive verbs. The most frequent active verbs are *seem, appear, claim*. The most frequent passive verbs are *be believed, be known, be reported, be found, be rumored, be alleged, be said,* and the expression *be supposed to*.
> Shakespeare's plays **appear to have been enjoyed** by Queen Elizabeth I.
> Shakespeare **is believed to have been born** in 1564.

Complete the sentences in the article using the verbs given. Sometimes the first verb in each pair can be present or past. Each verb phrase has a passive perfect infinitive.

The movie *Anonymous* reignited interest in the English poet and playwright Shakespeare. The plot of the movie focuses on the debate, which _____ (seem / not /resolve), about whether Shakespeare wrote his own plays. Few records of his personal life _____ (appear / keep), which makes verifying his work difficult. Here are some of the issues on which scholars _____ (seem / divide) for many years.

1. Shakespeare's plays _____ (believe / compose) in collaboration with other authors.
2. Secret codes about the political climate of the time _____ (report / hide) in his plays.
3. The plays _____ (rumor / write) by his rival, Christopher Marlowe. In one study, identical word patterns _____ (find / use) by both writers.
4. In the movie *Anonymous*, the plays _____ (allege / write) by Edward de Vere, Earl of Oxford. A well-traveled lawyer, de Vere _____ (report / kidnap) by pirates and left on the shores of Denmark, which was supposedly the inspiration for *Hamlet*. However, this event _____ (seem / not / find) in written sources used for the play, which raises the question: How did Shakespeare know some of the details? Many of the other places that de Vere visited _____ (say / include) in Shakespeare's plays.
5. Supporters of Shakespeare as the author of the plays dismiss these theories, saying that they _____ (appear / give) too much credibility.

2 would rather

> - After *would rather*, you can use a passive base form.
> *He would rather **be remembered** for his philanthropy. He'd rather **not be remembered** for his crimes.*
>
> - Notice the patterns in comparisons.
> Passive + active: *He would rather **be killed** than **give up** his beliefs.*
> Passive + passive: *He'd rather **be loved** than **(be) respected**.*

Read the article and complete it with passive base forms of the verbs given.

In law enforcement, many crimes go unsolved and sometimes remain a mystery. Not so in the case of a Florida grandmother. While she would probably rather _____ (know) for her good deeds than _____ (remember) for her crimes, this "pillar of the community" shocked neighbors when she was arrested 34 years *after* her crimes were committed. She was sent to jail, and while it's understandable that anyone would rather _____ (give) probation than _____ (sentence) to five years in prison, the woman shocked the community again. Two months later, she escaped from prison, obviously feeling that she would really much rather _____ (leave) alone to live her life out of jail than _____ (serve) a prison sentence.

Unit 12, Lesson A — Grammar extra
Common verbs, adjectives, and nouns + object + -ing

- Here are some common verbs, adjectives, and nouns that introduce object + -ing patterns.

Verbs +	keep, appreciate, remember, leave, mind, get, hear, see, feel, watch
prepositions	hear about, listen to, worry about, result in, count on, depend on, think of, insist on
Adjectives +	interested in, tired of, sick of, supportive of, worried about, wrong with, responsible
prepositions	for, excited about, (un)comfortable with, aware of, serious about, good about, happy with / about, fine with, grateful for, crucial / critical to, crazy about
Nouns +	picture / photo / video of, thought of, report of, questions of / about, probability
prepositions	of, possibility of, chance(s) of, danger of, worries about, way of

I **remember** my father **giving** me a lot of advice.
But he also said, "I'm not **responsible for** you **repeating** my mistakes!"
I said, "There's no **chance of** me **doing** that!"

A Read the advice to parents of young adults. Rewrite the underlined parts of the sentences, using a pattern in the chart. You may need to delete or add words and change the verb forms.

After college – what then?

happy about their adult children moving back
Many parents are happy if their adult children move back into their home after college, and in many families, it's expected that they will do so. For others, though, the thought that their offspring will return home raises worries that their privacy will be invaded. What's more, while parents mostly want to be supportive so their children will find their way in life, there is a limit to the financial support they can offer.

1. If you're uncomfortable that your adult children might live at home, then say so. Say you don't mind if they live with you for a fixed period of time. Then insist that they move out.

2. Set ground rules from the outset. If children count on the fact that their parents will do everything for them, they may never do anything for themselves. Parents often see that their children are taking advantage of them. You don't want this to leave you in a situation where you feel resentful toward your children, so speak up. There's nothing wrong if they want to do things their own way, but they are in *your* home.

3. If the chances that your adult children will be financially dependent on you for a long time are high, then you should probably do something about it. You need to be serious so your kids will figure out how to manage their own money. Don't pay for everything.

4. The probability that unemployed children will remain unemployed is higher if you don't insist that they pay their own way. Don't worry if your children go without luxuries or even basics. There's a good possibility that they will be more motivated to find work if they can't buy the things they want.

5. If your adult children are adamant that you should support them, be firm. Say you are not responsible for the fact that they need to find work. On the other hand, say you would appreciate the fact that they do chores and work around the home in return for rent.

B Look at the sentences you rewrote. Choose six and make them more formal by using a possessive determiner (*their, your, 's*) before the *-ing* form.

Many parents are happy about their adult children's moving back home after college.

Unit 12, Lesson B — Grammar extra

1 More on reflexive pronouns

- Reflexive pronouns are often used after *find, protect, defend, consider / see, call, ask, kill, describe, identify, pride . . . on* (= be proud), *distance, express, reinvent, introduce, see for*.
  He **prides himself on** being an expert, but even he **found himself** "dating" a piece of software.

- *Itself* is often used after *in, lend,* and *speak for*.
  Identifying who you are writing to is a problem **in itself**. (= without considering other issues)
  This tale of Internet deception **lends itself** to a movie adaptation. (= is suitable for)
  His willingness to talk openly about the event **speaks for itself**. (= is clear)

> **Common errors**
> You don't need a reflexive pronoun after *apologize, complain, develop, feel, relax, remember*.
> **I felt** unhappy at first, but then I began to **relax**. (NOT . . . ~~felt myself~~ . . . ~~relax myself~~)

Read the article and complete it with reflexive pronouns. If one is not needed, write an X.

Even if you pride _____ on being a good judge of character, when it comes to online relationships, ask _____ if you are sure about who you are in touch with. Meeting people online is a challenge in _____. Many of us who have found _____ in a problematic online relationship say we didn't see it coming – even those of us who call _____ experts. People often reinvent _____ online, and email doesn't lend _____ to getting to know someone well. You may have to protect _____ from dangerous people. Take my friend Ana, who considers _____ a cautious person. This guy introduced _____ via a dating site and described _____ as caring *and* single. The relationship developed _____, but on their first real date, he apologized _____ for being evasive, which in _____ was a warning sign. How the story ends speaks for _____. He turned out to be married. She distanced _____ from him, but he started turning up at her home. She couldn't relax _____ and complained _____ to the police.

2 Referring to unknown people

- If you refer back to an unknown person, you can use *he or she, him or her,* and *himself or herself*. People often say *they, their,* and *themselves*, especially after *everyone*, etc., but do not write this.
  It is up to the person **himself or herself** whether to see a doctor when **he or she** needs to.
  Everybody needs sympathy when **their** problems affect their health.

> **Common errors**
> Don't use *itself* for people or to refer back to plural nouns.
> The patient was in fact a doctor **herself**. (NOT The patient was a doctor ~~itself~~.)
> My friends do online dating **themselves**. (NOT My friends do online dating ~~itself~~.)

Complete the sentences. Then rewrite sentences 1–4 as you might tell a friend in a conversation.

1. Everyone should make sure that *his or her* personal details are not online.
   Everyone should make sure their personal details are not online.
2. An online dater can always ask for a background check if _____ wishes to.
3. Nobody should let _____ guard down when they meet _____ date. Meet several times, ask to meet _____ friends, and find out where _____ works.
4. Everybody should ask _____ if _____ is a good judge of character. If not, ask a friend to come along and meet your new date.
5. People can protect _____ by meeting in a public place.

Grammar extra **167**

Illustration credits

77: (cartoon) Liza Donnelly/Cambridge University Press; **93:** (cartoon) Liza Donnelly/Cambridge University Press; **97:** (cartoon) Liza Donnelly/Cambridge University Press; **107:** (cartoon) Liza Donnelly/Cambridge University Press; **117:** (cartoon) Liza Donnelly/Cambridge University Press; **127:** (cartoon) Liza Donnelly/Cambridge University Press

Photography credits

Back cover: © vovan/Shutterstock; **74:** (top right from left to right) © Thinkstock, © Casarsa/istockphoto, © daniel rodriguez/istockphoto, (middle left) © Thinkstock;
75: © AP Photo/The Day, Sean D. Elliot; **76:** (top left) © Oleksandr Koval/Shutterstock, (top right) © Andrea Morini/Thinkstock, (background) © tukkki/Shutterstock; **78:** Cambridge University Press; **79:** (top) Cambridge University Press, (middle right) © Kyu Oh/istockphoto; **80:** (top right) © Patrik Giardino/Media Bakery, (background) © Fancy/Media Bakery; **81:** © By Ian Miles-Flashpoint Pictures/Alamy; **83:** © Thinkstock; **84:** (top right from left to right) © kmiragay/Fotolia, © Maxiphoto/istockphoto, © Tim Graham/Alamy, (middle from left to right) © pictore/iStockphoto, © Ralf Hettler/iStockphoto, © Thinkstock, © Pantheon/SuperStock; **85:** (top to bottom) © Thinkstock, © Lightroom Photos/NASA/Photoshot/Newscom, © Mary Evans Picture Library/Alamy, © Georgios Kollidas/istockphoto; **86:** (top to bottom) © Andrew Howe/iStockphoto, © Erlend Kvalsvik/iStockphoto, © Belinda Images/SuperStock, (background) © Itana/Shutterstock; **87:** (top to bottom) © AP Photo/Elise Amendola, © Bettmann/CORBIS; **88:** Cambridge University Press; **89:** (top) Cambridge University Press, (bottom) © Paolo Cipriani/iStockphoto; **90:** © Science and Society/SuperStock, (background) © nortivision/Shutterstock; **91:** (left to right) © Duncan Walker/istockphoto, © Jan Kratochvila/istockphoto, © jupeart/Shutterstock,© Thinkstock, © Thinkstock; **94:** (top right from left to right) © Nomad_Soul/Shutterstock, © Sue Cunningham Photographic/Alamy, © Fedorov Oleksiy/Shutterstock, (middle left from top to bottom) © Stock Connection/SuperStock, © Stock Connection/SuperStock (middle right from top to bottom) © Thinkstock, © Thinkstock; **95:** © scibak/iStockphoto; **96:** (top to bottom) © Art Kowalsky/Alamy, © UIG/Getty Images, (background) © Robert Adrian Hillman/Shutterstock; **97:** (left to right) © Luboslav Tiles/Shutterstock, © Marat Dupri/Shutterstock, © Paul Dymond/Alamy, © Bloomberg/Getty Images; **98:** Cambridge University Press; **99:** Cambridge University Press; **100:** (bottom left) © AFP/Getty Images, (right from top to bottom) © Vladislav Ociacia/istockphoto, © REUTERS/Christian Charisius/Newscom, © Alperium/iStockphoto, (background) © one AND only/Shutterstock; **101:** © epa european pressphoto agency b.v./Alamy; **103:** © auremar/Shutterstock; **106:** (top right from left to right) © pictafolio/istockphoto, © Karin Hildebrand Lau/Shutterstock, © ChameleonsEye/Shutterstock, (middle, top to bottom) © Minden Pictures/SuperStock, © tillsonburg/iStockphoto, © eurobanks/Shutterstock, © Thinkstock; **108:** (top right) © Hocus Focus Studio/istockphoto, (middle) © Feng Yu/Shutterstock, (background) © Skylines/Shutterstock; **109:** (left from top to bottom) © Juanmonino/istockphoto, © zhang bo/istockphoto, © Ann Marie Kurtz/istockphoto, (torn paper) © Robyn Mackenzie/Shutterstock; **110:** Cambridge University Press; **111:** (top) Cambridge University Press, (bottom) © AFP/Getty Images; **112:** (middle right) © justasc/Shutterstock, (middle) © Ice-Storm/Shutterstock, (background) © essxboy/iStockphoto; **113:** © Thinkstock; **116:** (top right from left to right) © Moviestore collection Ltd/Alamy, © Zdorov Kirill Vladimirovich/Shutterstock, © Hemis/Alamy, (bottom middle) © pockygallery/Shutterstock, (background) © sgame/Shutterstock; **118:** (left) © Presselect/Alamy, (background) © AF archive/Alamy; **119:** © agencyby/iStockphoto; **120:** (left middle) Cambridge University Press, (bottom right) © Thinkstock; **121:** (top) Cambridge University Press, (middle) © Luis Louro/Shutterstock, © Steve Debenport/iStockphoto; **122:** (left) © Greg Balfour Evans/Alamy, (right) © AP Photo/Jens Meyer, (frame) © Julia Ivantsova/Shutterstock, (background) © Nino Cavalier/Shutterstock; **126:** (top right from left to right) © Vasiliy Yakobchuk/istockphoto, © bikeriderlondon/Shutterstock, (middle from left to right) © Yuri Arcurs/Shutterstock, © auremar/Shutterstock, © Thinkstock; **128:** (top left) © ImageZoo/Alamy, (background) © art4all/Shutterstock; **129:** © Rogue Pictures/courtesy Everett Collection; **130:** Cambridge University Press; **131:** (top) Cambridge University Press, (bottom) © LUNAMARINA/istockphoto; **132:** © Thinkstock, (background) © DVARG/Shutterstock; **133:** © annedde/istockphoto; **158:** © Archive Pics/Alamy

Text credits

The authors and publishers acknowledge the following sources of copyright material and are grateful for the permissions granted. While every effort has been made, it has not always been possible to identify the sources of all the material used, or to trace all copyright holders. If any omissions are brought to our notice, we will be happy to include the appropriate acknowledgements on reprinting.

80 Data used by permission of Pew Research Center's Internet & American Life Project.
136 Information on women in the workplace used from the U.S. Census Bureau (www.census.gov/hhes/socdemo/education/data/cps/2010/tables.html) and from a 2009 study conducted by N. Scott Taylor of the University of New Mexico.

Corpus

Development of this publication has made use of the Cambridge English Corpus (CEC). The CEC is a computer database of contemporary spoken and written English, which currently stands at over one billion words. It includes British English, American English, and other varieties of English. It also includes the Cambridge Learner Corpus, developed in collaboration with the University of Cambridge ESOL Examinations. Cambridge University Press has built up the CEC to provide evidence about language use that helps produce better language teaching materials.